"It is certainly high noon for Corpi, an award-winning author of numerous books of poetry and fiction and one of the first Mexican American writers to gain recognition in this country. But this collection . . . represents her dawn."
— *Críticas* on *Palabras de mediodía / Noon Words*

" . . . dazzlingly evocative prose . . . some original and highly charged moments . . . Corpi expands the genre with this work."   — *Publishers Weekly* on *Eulogy for a Brown Angel*

" . . . the bloody conclusion adds an extra wallop to the convoluted goings-on . . . worthwhile mystery reading."
— *Kirkus Reviews* on *Eulogy for a Brown Angel*

" . . . a twisting story line that confounds her intelligent detective and the reader at every turn. This will please readers looking for a fast-paced tale with a Hispanic cultural background."
— *Library Journal* on *Death at Solstice*

Confessions of a
Book Burner

PERSONAL ESSAYS + STORIES

*Querida Aldrea, May
these stories & ideas &
& opinions serve as
bridge between us to*

LUCHA CORPI *continue*

Abrazos *sharing
thenoir*

Lucha Corpi

22 sept 2018

Arte Público Press
Houston, Texas

Confessions of a Book Burner: Personal Essays and Stories is funded in part by grants from the city of Houston through the Houston Arts Alliance.

Recovering the past, creating the future

Arte Público Press
University of Houston
4902 Gulf Fwy, Bldg 19, Rm 100
Houston, Texas 77204-2004

Cover art by Patricia Rodriguez, "The Burning Heart"
Cover design by Mora Des¡gn

14 15 16 17 18 19 20 21   10 9 8 7 6 5 4 3 2 1

TABLE OF CONTENTS

In memoriam: to my parents, Miguel Ángel Corpi and Victoria Constantino Ramos, and my gradmother, Nicolasa Aguirre

And to:

My son Arturo Enrique Hernández, my daughter-in-law Naomi Madell and my grandchildren, Kiara, Nikolas and Kamille Hernández

My husband, Carlos Medina Gonzales

My siblings, Víctor Miguel, María Concepción, Miguel Ángel, Guillermo Alonso, Jorge Alberto, Francisco Javier and Luis Enrique Corpi Constantino, and their respective families

My niece Frieda Molina, her husband Craig Howard and my grandnephew-nieto, Quincy E. Howard

REMEMBRANCE, POETRY AND STORYTELLING

NINETEEN FIFTY-TWO was a frightening year, yet one of the most memorable in my life. I discovered poetry and learned to memorize poems and recite them in public. It was also the year I began to remember my dreams, especially my recurring nightmares. Learning poems or songs by heart and being able to recall them at will were activities that brought me great pleasure. Memorizing multiplication tables wasn't exactly a thrilling activity. According to my parents, however, learning them was a life skill that would come in handy every day of my life. But what good was there in remembering nightmares? I tried to figure out how remembering happened, sure that if I could get that knowledge, I would also find out how to unlearn terrifying memories.

One day, I was watching my friend Marta ride her brother Paco's bicycle backwards without looking back or at the mirror. At times, she would land on her butt. After rubbing it, she would again mount the bike. It occurred to me that maybe un-remembering was similar to learning how to pedal a bicycle in reverse but with eyes always fixed on the road ahead. I would simply follow the same course, first forward then backwards. But didn't that mean that I would have to make an effort to remember the bumps on my path in order to avoid them? Just like learning multiplication tables, always the same result, I thought in frustration. In a few weeks, my friend Marta had mastered the reverse-pedaling skill, without further damage to her butt. On the other hand, I wasn't any closer to figuring out how remembering or un-remembering happened, and my nightmares still plagued my nights and days.

Decades later, I would smile as I recalled the foolish notions of the child in me, who could only sense the importance of memory, or its undoing, as a means to survival. Studying the inner workings of my unconscious and subliminal minds for a story I was writing, I became aware that sensual and sensory memories share a space in the unconscious mind, where metaphors and dreams alike take substance from the deeper layers of intuition, emotions, sensations and perceptions of colors. Sometimes, these random memories trigger the release of experiences associated with them and clustered together to form a poem or to provide the setting in a story with the colors it needed to create mood.

In many ways, our sense of vision is the most discriminating, and we largely rely on it for survival, but nature regales us with a colorful world from the first moment our eyes open to light until they shut it out for the last time. Thus, it seems only natural that colors are among the earliest subliminal memories most of us have and hold onto from infancy to adulthood. More often than we care to admit, they determine our choices in many subtle and insidious ways, and for reasons of which we are hardly aware.

In *Canícula: Snapshots of a Girlhood en la Frontera,* Norma Elia Cantú uses a series of photos as the focal points of narratives and stories about the narrator—perhaps herself—at different ages, alone or with friends or members of her immediate and large extended families, who live on both sides of the

United States-Mexico border. Cantú calls this multi-layered rich narrative "ethnography." One of the snapshots shows a baby in a stroller being pushed by her grandmother. The narrator-writer says about it: "My memory for everything but the stroller is like the photo, black and white; the stroller is the blue of my winter coat when I was sixteen. When I saw the coat on the rack at J.C. Penney's, I had to have it . . . Years later I realized it reminded me of that stroller. Painted blue, made of metal and wood. I remember it well . . . "

Cantú's snapshot text is a vivid example of how the unconscious mind shapes our sensory perceptions of colors and influences our predilections. Eventually, these unconscious memories inform and re-form the stories we have lived and told. Thus, at times, our reactions to colors depend on the circumstances at the time we first come to perceive them as being positive or negative. At other times, we learn not to fear or to consider a certain color normal or tolerable, simply by the preponderance of that color in our immediate environment.

Since I was born in the tropics, inescapably but fortunately for me, my unconscious mind was flooded with green the very first instant my eyes opened to light. My oldest and first memory is of green. Thereafter, anything green became an object of contemplation everywhere in my small tropical world:

Slithering green and mimetic green sunbathing on a blade of grass, or a tree branch—loud parrot green—lemon green—lime green—ceiba green—golden-avocado green—green-papaya and green-mango greens—cool green of tranquil river pools. Green the light filtering through the canopy of tropical trees, of leaves floating downstream after a storm. Green the aroma of banana leaves wrapped over tamales de presa or around Mexican beef barbecue baked in underground earth ovens. Green, as hope is an evergreen, like it was in my father's hazel eyes as he sang me to sleep.

If you open my closet, you'll hardly see any green garments among the clothes there. But my writing space, even when it has been only a narrow table in a corner of the living room, has always faced a window with natural greenery beyond it. Green is the way my spirit spells constancy and harmony. It's at once the familiar present and the connective tissue between my past and future.

My own sense of self as an individual is as fluid as the sound of the wind moving through foliage, and teeming with possibilities in the deep pools of streams and estuaries, beneath all the greens of my memory. My poetry flows from one of those streams. But the writer in me learned her craft by navigating another current, the stream of the oral tradition of storytelling.

In Jáltipan, Veracruz, every family had a number of storytellers of both genders. They were usually the older relatives—not to say that younger people weren't also fond of telling a story. The difference between the older and younger storytellers was the subject of their stories, and the treatment of them. In my family, both my father and mother told us stories. With few exceptions, my dad's stories were humorous and told about his and his friends' misadventures in search of buried treasure, and as a member of a short-lived theater company in Jáltipan. My mother's life stories were for the most part sad and underscored by her tears and sighs. But the storyteller per excellence was my paternal grandmother, Nicolasa Aguirre—Abuelita Nico—who was able to bring together all kinds of disparate elements and make familial and other stories work as oral units at once seamless and self-sustaining, scary or amusing yet educational, and dealing with subjects of interest to a varied, larger group of people.

Images of my grandmother braiding her hair, singing, looking at treasured mementos in her cedar trunk, talking with my father or mother, my aunt Pancha or cousins, answering my questions while she worked a wire to make or fix a piece of jewelry, feeding the chickens in the backyard, drinking hot black coffee, slicing pomelos in half and squeezing their juice out, then adding it to pre-sweetened water to accompany the afternoon meal. I can feel the softness of her cotton garments and smell their clean fragrance, just as when I used to rest my head on her chest and listen to the crescendo of her heartbeat as she talked about the impossibility of attaining true justice in this world.

If I sit in absolute silence, I can hear the sound of her cascading laughter when something tickled her fancy and a bit of wickedness in her soft chuckles when she talked about her own or other people's foibles. I can also see the frown and hear the sigh when she looked into the bottom of the cedar chest in her room. I wondered what it was that she kept hidden there. Was it the memory of hooded and unruly creatures, like those in my nightmares, perhaps, lying in ambush at the bottom of the cedar chest her heart had become? Was it the flitting memory of her mother, who died young, leaving her heart orphaned, or perhaps the memory of Víctor Corpi, my dad's dad? I never knew because she never told me the story of her life with him.

Sometimes, when I can't find my way out of a problem or mend a snag in the writing, I purposely bring to mind the way she told various kinds of stories. Some were linear, others uncoiled horizontally like a wire spring, while still others spiraled down to a dark place where fear reigned seemingly unchallenged, but also where goodness somehow always managed to thrive. I am grateful I was in her company frequently for nineteen years and am able to recall images and conversations at will.

For the story of my maternal grandmother, Manuela Ramos, who died seventeen years before I was born, I've had to rely on my mother, whose memories of her mother are the aggregate of only a few of her own plus other family members' recollections of her mother. When I think of my grandmother Manuela, it is the picture of my mother I recall. *She twiddles her thumbs. She looks like she's just tasted a lemon. My mom always does that when she tells us how she lost her mother at age five. How she and my dad want the best for us, their children. We are the most important people in the world to them. Nothing can be worse than to feel like an orphan when your own father is alive but doesn't come to see you. She looks at my dad. He tries to smile, but his eyes get teary. My dad loves my mom very much. Remember this, my mother says: family is everything. I look at my brother, Víctor. He's crying, too. We sympathize with mom. We don't want her to cry, but she does it every time. I cannot understand why. We love her. My dad loves her. Isn't our love for her enough? She insists on telling us her sad story. I don't want to listen, but I do. I do listen.*

In 1923, Manuela gave birth to Victoria, my mother. My aunt Ole arrived three years later, and my aunt Hilda two years after Ole's birth. Baby Hilda survived the ordeal of childbirth, but Manuela died. My mother was a little over five years of age by then. They lived in Ixhuatlán, a municipality in southern Veracruz, near the town of Acayucan, where the Constantinos, my grandfather's siblings, *tías* Adelita and Juanita, and *tío* Gilberto, lived.

My grandfather, el Chato Constantino, mourned Manuela's death and contemplated taking his daughters to live with him. He was overwhelmed by the responsibility since he knew nothing about bringing up girls, what with their female problems and having to be protected and supported. Had they been sons, well, that would have been a different story. The girls stayed with their maternal grandmother for a few months. Then my grandfather took the girls to Acayucan to stay with his youngest, unmarried sister, my grandaunt, Adela, and talked her into taking care of his girls. Had she lived in modern times, being in her early thirties, Adela would have been young enough to marry and still bear children. Given the life expectancy at the time, she was already considered middle-aged, therefore, an "old maid." Men preferred wives much younger than them. Younger women were more malleable and physically better able to take care of their ailing husbands in their old age. Sometimes, men waited for the girls to have their first menstrual period and shortly thereafter married them, with the girls' parents' permission, of course, but not with their child-brides' consent.

Perhaps responding to her maternal instinct or because she truly loved the girls, Aunt Adela agreed to look after my mom and my aunts. El Chato provided some financial support, but contact with his daughters was sporadic, partly because his business took him away from home for many days at a time. Many years after Manuela's death, he'd finally taken a second wife in Jáltipan and had two children with her. Whenever Adela reported what his daughters were going through emotionally, how much they needed him, how difficult it became for them when he was late with the money he sent, he simply shoved his sister's concerns aside. No one was going to tell el Chato what to do, or how to conduct his affairs.

Teary-eyed, my mother used to tell us how hard her and her sisters' lives were. How unsympathetically people, including better-off relatives, behaved toward them, scolding them all the time, locking the pantry so the young girls—the "orphans"—would not "steal" their cousins' snacks. Even though my mother had a father, she felt as if she were really an orphan. Being the oldest, she also felt responsible for her sisters' care and emotional well-being, protecting them from school bullies, being their champion when anyone else mistreated or tried to humiliate them. Uncle Gilberto, el Chato's brother, was kind to them and made sure they had at least enough to eat.

Aunt Adela was a good surrogate mother and did the best she could for the girls. All of them finished elementary school. They learned to cook, keep house and make their own clothes. Adela made it possible for my mother to enroll in teacher-preparation and clerical vocational programs in Córdoba, a much larger city. She was sixteen when she graduated and was getting ready to look for a job, at either a school or an office, when el Chato summoned her to his side for the first time in her life. Perhaps he wanted to get to know her better, Aunt Adela told my mom.

My mother didn't want to be away from her sisters and from the only parent she had ever known, but she agreed to move to Jáltipan. Soon, she found out el Chato's main reason for wanting her close by. She was to look after her younger half-brother and half-sister and teach them everything she knew. After all, it was time that she paid him back for the education he'd made possible for her. My mother wanted a chance to live with her father, perhaps to find out if he really loved her and cared what happened to her, despite his earlier neglect. She moved to Jáltipan. Not long after settling in, she met my father at a party she attended with a couple of new girlfriends. Living in the same small town, my grandfather had had occasion to meet Abuelita Nico and had heard things about my father. What he had heard didn't make a difference to him until my father became interested in my mother.

At age 27, my dad was nine years older than my mother and was also the most sought-after bachelor in town. A self-made man, and a great dancer, he was also affable, charming, and had a good sense of humor. He wasn't a drinker or prone to violence. In fact, he would always try to talk feuding individuals out of a fight. No doubt, parents of teen-aged daughters in town thought he would make an excellent husband and father. He had a secondary education, and whatever else he knew he had taught himself by reading or apprenticing on his own—one of his lifelong trademarks. His having a steady job and already moving up the ladder at work was a great incentive for parents to, subtly and overtly, let him know that he'd be welcomed as their son-in-law.

My grandfather's objections to my dad were many, but he summarized them in the single expression: "*Es un gallo ya muy jugado*" (He's a rooster who's already been around a lot). When my dad began to show interest in my mother, the whole town watched their every move. Often, other young women, competing for my father's heart, would stand behind my mom and pull her hair or ruffle her clothes as a warning for her to stay away from him. They made comments about my dad's former love interests around town. In short, they tried every trick in the book to make her reject him. But my dad had fallen in love with my mom, and she with him. So he proposed marriage to her only twenty-four days into their formal courtship. As tradition required, he talked to el Chato and asked for my mom's hand in marriage.

At first, my grandfather came up with an objection: "I don't have any money to pay for a wedding." My dad countered: "I've been working for many years and I have managed to save some money. I will pay for everything, including her wedding gown." The game went on until my grandfather perfunctorily stated, "I don't approve of your family."

My father said nothing to that final statement, turned around and left. He made sure my mom could live for the rest of her life with the decision he asked her to make. Despite her father's efforts to keep them apart, my mom went on with her plans to marry my dad. They set a date for their wedding, hoping that my grandfather would finally come to terms with the inevitable. He didn't. On the eve of my parents' wedding, el Chato drank one too many and came home with a crow bar.

"I'd rather see you dead, than married to a son of Nicolasa Aguirre," he announced. He lanced the floor a couple of feet from her feet with the crow bar. My mother ran out of the house and took refuge with a family in town that was very fond of her. She sent a telegram to my uncle Gilberto Constantino in Acayucan asking him to go to Jáltipan and give her away. He showed up, and the next day my mom and dad were married.

Even though they both lived in Jáltipan, my grandfather and my mother did not talk to each other for years, not even after my brother Víctor and I were born. He was as "stubborn as his mules," my mother used to say, although she herself didn't make an effort to reach out to him either. He lived across from the marketplace and would watch my brother and me from his front door whenever our *nana* Paula took us shopping. One day, he decided to approach Paula and asked her to take us to his home. He promised to give her kilos of rice, corn and beans and bunches of bananas in exchange for the favor. Paula agreed. The memory of that visit with my grandfather is the only one I'm able to recognize and accept as mine:

I'm looking at him, a man in a white sleeveless undershirt and black pants. Thick eyelashes hedge irises the color of brown-veined emeralds. Straight black eyebrows, low cheekbones and thin lips frame a short and flat nose. People call him "el Chato" because of that flat nose. He doesn't smile or laugh. I feel the soft skin on his arms, in contrast with the rough, sandy hands that pick me up. He gives me a peeled tiny banana to eat. I show four fingers to tell him my age and say "cuatro—four," then pull my thumb out and add, "Casi cinco—almost five." He peels four more tiny bananas for me. They melt in my mouth like dulce de leche—milk candy. "Toyita—little Toya," he calls me, after my mother's nickname. He gives Víctor the marble-size balls of cocoa rolled in coconut and sugar my brother loves. El Chato calls my brother by the diminutive of my father's name: "Miguelito."

In this recollection of the day we visited my grandfather, I am certain I'm there. I have a sense of myself, but I cannot see my face, nor do I remember the clothes or shoes I wore. I see my fingers. I see the tiny fruit. I see el Chato. The only way I could have seen my face and my clothes, and being in the arms of el Chato, would have been possible if I had seen our images reflected on glass or a mirror in the room, or in a photo of the reunion. There was no mirror and no camera, and my face is not there. To the extent that I can, I trust that this is my own memory and not what someone else has told me about my grandfather.

The rest of my grandfather's story, as told here, is family lore. Some relatives believe that this story my mother told us is not entirely true. What part of any story that has gone through rumination and reflection, or that imagination has chewed and spat out, is or isn't entirely true? Since the events described happened long before I was born, I cannot attest to their truth. All I can do is to quote my mother, who believed this episode in el Chato's life was true. According to her:

Diódoro "el Chato" Constantino, my maternal grandfather, was a grain broker and often traded for dry goods with the *serranos*, mountain folk who lived in remote villages in the coastal range of Mexico's Eastern Sierra Madre. Traveling in the sierra in the 1930s implied spending the night anyplace safe. Most people planned their journeys so they would be close to or in a village by sundown. The southern half of the state of Veracruz is on the Tropic of Cancer, thus closer to the equator. Days and nights there are almost equally long year round. Depending on the season, sunsets in the Jáltipan of my childhood were consistently between six and seven in the evening; the sun rose any time from five to six in the morning.

In the sierra, it was a good idea to have found shelter by six in the evening. Darkness was the dominion of wild jungle cats, coyotes and other night predators looking for supper, whether human or animal. Village people usually opened their barns to travelers or welcomed them to share floor space on *petates* (grass mats) or cots in a single large room detached from the main house; sometimes free of charge, at others in exchange for grain or other goods.

Over the years, I heard many stories about el Chato's dealings with the *serranos*, who were fierce, rugged people. Like most children, I loved hearing scary stories, as long as I could take refuge in an adult's arms when fear became unbearable. One of those stories about el Chato involved his dealings with a family of very strange *serranos* on a very dark new-moon night, on his way back from Mount San Martín, a dormant volcano at the southernmost tip of the coastal Sierra Madre.

Night was falling fast when el Chato reached an isolated village he'd never visited before. He'd been away from home for almost two weeks. Looking at the few stars already shining made him homesick. Although he would have preferred reaching flat terrain, he was exhausted and the grumbling in his stomach reminded him he hadn't eaten since noon. If he left at dawn the next day, he could be setting foot on the lower tropical savannahs by that day's end.

El Chato knocked on the door of a home on the outskirts of the village and asked the lady of the house if he and his three mules could spend the night there, or if not, at least be allowed to wash up and rest a little. She smiled but didn't ask for his name or give hers. Trying to sweeten the deal, he offered the lady of the house a kilo each of rice and coffee beans. She not only accepted the exchange for sleeping space, but invited him to have supper with her and her husband in a half hour. The aroma emanating from the kitchen was enticing.

Once his beasts were fed and their burdens removed, he went back to the house. His mouth watered when the smell of fresh-made corn tortillas and roasted peppers reached his nostrils. He asked for permission to wash up. The lady pointed at some place down the breezeway. She handed him a candle to light his way to a small washroom at the end of it.

As he moved down the breezeway, he sniffed the air. The *serranos* had probably slaughtered a steer or a pig and were getting ready to dry or cure the meat. The pungent smell of blood seemed to float out of the supply room. His curiosity got the better of him and he could not resist pushing the door open and shedding light into the room. Along the walls, there were large baskets full of different grains, dried legumes and unshelled peanuts. He glimpsed at two carcasses hanging from meat hooks, then gasped and took two steps back. His breath was quick and felt hot in his throat and chest. His hand trembled as he raised the candle. Half of a disemboweled man hung from one of the meat hooks. El Chato gagged and clutched his stomach. With barely enough breath to blow out the candle, he staggered out onto the breezeway and made it to the open wash area just in time to spit out a bitter mouthful that burned his throat and tongue as if it were acid. He rinsed his mouth and splashed cold water on his head, torso and arms. He washed his feet and legs. Since it would have been inappropriate to remove his garments, he could only wipe his crotch and butt with the same large square of wet terry cloth he had used for drying himself.

His body warmed up and he stopped shaking. His breathing became almost normal. In all the years he had traveled in the sierra, he had heard of cannibalism in the villages, but had never come face to face with it. Forcing himself to dismiss the thought, he struggled to gather his wits about him. His survival would depend on what he did next. His mind crowded with all sorts of ways to bow out and leave without arousing suspicion from his hostess. However, no matter how he looked at his predicament, it came down to eating a meal perhaps made with human flesh or risking the possibility of being those *serranos'* main course the next day. He took deep breaths before stepping back into the kitchen, where the lady and her husband already waited for him. He handed her the small sacks of dry goods he'd promised. Her husband offered El Chato a shot of sugarcane *aguardiente*. He couldn't risk saying no, so he raised his glass to thank his hosts for their hospitality, drained half the liquor in it and sipped the rest.

El Chato threw a quick glance at the steaming soup in his bowl. Small pieces of shredded dark-pink meat and small corn-dough and vegetable dumplings floated in a rich yellow broth. Had he not seen the contents of the supply room, he would have already slurped a taste of what looked like "hen" soup. Praying to a higher power that it was really chicken soup, he held his breath as he gulped down each spoonful until he finished his meal. Praising the lady's culinary skills, he thanked her and her husband again for their hospitality.

After supper, his host and hostess talked briefly with el Chato about his business. They never told him their names; not once did they ask for his. They always called him "*arriero*—carrier." He kept himself from saying where exactly he was from. They asked him to stop by on his next visit if he had any legumes, peanuts or cocoa beans to trade. The lady of the house showed him to a spot near the wood stove, before they retired for the night.

El Chato spread his *petate* on the floor and placed his machete next to him under the light serape he always carried with him. He didn't undress nor did he take his shoes off. Racing thoughts kept his heart beating hard as he lay under the blanket. Seized by alternate spells of tremors and nausea, he listened intently to the night sounds of the house until he heard the *serranos'* loud and steady snores. Quietly he gathered his belongings and scurried out of the house to the corral, where he stuck his fingers deep into his throat to induce vomiting. He rinsed his mouth with a swig of water, then gulped down a swig of rum from a flask he always carried with him. He strapped his belongings onto one of the mules and tied the other two beasts to the first.

Hauling his mule train down a snaky single-file path off the main mountain road proved to be a very difficult task in the new-moon darkness. Howls and growls in the distance did not deter him from his goal, but hours passed before he allowed himself to stop. He poured some water into a large bowl for the animals and into an old tin cup for himself. As he drank, he looked up at the most beautiful starry sky he'd ever seen. The whole Milky Way spread out like a shimmering black shawl above him. The Southern Cross pointed the way home. He broke down and cried. When he and his mules finally reached the tropical savannas, the sun was beginning its descent again, but his home was still a night's journey away. He didn't stop at the usual watering holes to talk with other carriers or grain brokers.

El Chato arrived home when his family was still asleep. He went into the washroom, bathed himself thoroughly with cold water and rubbed his teeth and tongue with bicarbonate. He still could not get rid of the bitter taste in his mouth. Even though he tried not to think of his experience at the serranos' house, the image of their victim hanging from a hook haunted him.

Sitting on the floor, his blanket wrapped around his shoulders, el Chato had a mug of warm orange blossom tea and a while later fell asleep, only to be awakened by a scream. He jumped to his feet, wielding his machete in the air. His wife swiftly backtracked to the kitchen door, her hand over her mouth to muffle a second scream. When he put his machete down, his wife, speechless, began to push him to their bedroom. His eyes opened wide as he looked at himself in a mirror there. The white of his eyeballs and the skin on his face, neck and arms were jaundiced. The yellow tint stuck to his skin for the next three weeks. "*Susto*—shock," the town healers told him. His liver had suffered as a result of his extremely frightening experience in the sierra. The recommended rituals for *susto* and the *mal de ojo*—evil eye—were cleansings and herbal or root infusions. The treatments were successful, but this liver condition, aggravated over the years by my grandfather's Saturday night drinking binges, would eventually take his life. As he faced the last year of his life, he reached out to my mother, and they made their peace.

It's only a matter of hours. El Chato's dying, my mother tells my father. The night my grandfather dies, my mother takes my brother Víctor and me with her, and we rush to his side. My father stays home with my baby sister, Conchita. Death already waits by her father's bedside, my mom is told as we walk in. We are too young to understand fully what dying means, she tells us. She doesn't want us to see her father die. She leaves us in the living area and joins El Chato's wife, the town priest and other supplicants in her father's room.

Víctor and I look for ways to entertain ourselves. We have fun playing hide-and-seek in the grain room. In the living area of the house, the flickering flames of the many candles burning create silly or grotesque dancing silhouettes on the walls, and Víctor and I work our own shadows into the phantasmagoria. Exhausted and lulled by the din of prayers and laments, we finally fall asleep on a hard wooden bench just outside our grandfather's room.

A long pause in the recitation of prayers wakes me up. But it is the thunderous and constant pounding on the wooden door, and a horse's neighing and snorting, that makes my heart speed like a locomotive at full throttle. I open my mouth but no sound tumbles out. My brother wakes up, bolts to his feet, then backtracks to the bench, and gets a hold of my hand. We run to my mother's side.

The supplicants and the priest at el Chato's bedside cry out: "Dear Lord, don't let el diablo—the devil—take his soul!" The prayers grow louder. The candle flames flutter wildly, caught in the gusts of rapid breaths between prayers. The shadows on the wall dance frantically, arms outstretched, palms out begging for mercy for el Chato's soul. The horse strikes the door once more, then takes off down the dirt road. The sound of hooves dissolves in the distance. I look at my mom. She's crying. El Chato squeezes her hand, whispers a "forgive me." And he's gone.

For days after el Chato's burial, the town was abuzz with the rumor that *el diablo*, riding his black stallion, had tried to snatch away my grandfather's soul. Víctor and I asked my mother if what people were saying about the devil was true. After all, we'd been there and we'd heard the pounding at the door and the beast's neighs and snorts. My mother said the night rider was probably a man who held one of el Chato's IOUs. Upon hearing that my grandfather was dying, the night rider had paid a visit to the house, hoping to collect on the debt before it was too late. El Chato died, however, and death nullified his debt to the night visitor.

My mother, on the other hand, was left with the lifelong uncollectable emotional debt her father owed her. El Chato had asked for her forgiveness and she had absolved him of all guilt as he lay dying. But my mother didn't realize she had already been programmed by my grandfather's neglect to feel undeserving deep inside, and to react to that feeling by fighting her circumstances even harder than before.

Afraid of rejection throughout her life, she sought unconditional love and acceptance from everyone around her. She responded to her great need for social validation with raw emotions, like bruises barely visible underneath the skin yet painfully exacerbated at the slightest contact with cold or heat. My mom lashed out verbally or physically whenever she felt unloved, personally slighted or when her authority was questioned, and, of all her children, I seemed to trigger all of those negative emotions in her during my years at home. Except for my father's devotion and love, nothing else seemed to be enough to fill that emotional void in my mom's orphaned heart.

Naturally, for me, my maternal grandparents' life stories are like far-away galaxies with many of the stars already extinguished. Long before their brilliant light reached me, their legendary stellar energy trekked through the dark holes of many memories. There, their stories collected bits of memorialized truth and pixie dust and other galactic stuff as they were reshaped and refashioned with each telling and by each teller. I can only trust that there are more than bits of truth in what I've been told about Manuela Ramos and el Chato Constantino.

As I write these personal and familial stories to the best of my knowledge or recollection, as I elaborate on ideas and experiences, I am driven by the urgency to tell the truth as barely and skeletally as possible, "without much ado," as my son, Arturo, often reminds me. And yet, I know that the storyteller in me always wants to know and tell more than my mind is able to remember, to fill in the gaps with creative perceptions and to do the cosmetic repair work the narrative requires. So I constantly build word structures around the facts, much like the Mayans kept building larger pyramids over and around each smaller chamber to encase and preserve the less imposing original edifice in the center. Such is the nature of storytelling.

For the most part, I now trust myself to identify my own memories and, yet, I also know that the memories I recognize as truly mine are merely moments suspended in time, the gist of the events I've lived through, snippets of the conversations I've had with people in both my bicultural-bilingual lives. Such is the nature of remembrance.

The process of remembering is as elusive as that of writing a poem. If the poet or the *rememberer* doesn't seize that moment precisely when it happens and writes down or memorizes the poem or the details of an event, conversation or observation, what remain are mostly the sensual, physical and psychological manifestations or the feelings and emotions experienced at a particular moment in time. With those few elements, salvaged from the original experience, the poet might construct a poem or *the rememberer* another version of the original memory and, in the process, transcend the reality that earlier made urgent the writing of the poem or the recording of the remembrance.

My son, Arturo, who is a neuroscientist at the University of Houston, and I have often talked about the processes of memory in the acquisition and retention of languages, and the role of remembrance in poetry and storytelling as well. These conversations and my own observations have helped me realize that, contrary to what I've thought since I was a child, memory resides everywhere and nowhere in my mind. Links are established. Associations with other events, thoughts and sensory experiences are constantly being triggered and reinterpreted by my unconscious memory. Sometimes what I sense are only the feelings or the strong emotions negative experiences have left in me, and I am aware of how much more easily and readily I remember the pain rather than the joy in my life.

Once, as a child, I wanted to acquire the ability to unremember my nightmares and other unsettling experiences. After many years, I was successful in co-habiting and finally drawing up a mutual-aid agreement with the creatures in them. At that moment, it occurred to me that I could never get rid of my painful memories, but I could, instead, make a pact with myself to look at the knowledge I had gained by remembering them. Further, in the process of learning what the nature of remembrance is about, I had stumbled upon a way of identifying the memories that are truly my own, and to tell them apart from those related by someone else. The familial stories I have told here have become part of the collective consciousness and memory I share with many others. I have also learned that memory is not a warehouse where different and distinct memories are neatly stacked, color-coded and tagged by category, importance or date. They are not ready for total recall, for retrieval by reason or by intuition at any given time. Most certainly, I now know that my memories do not constitute a frame-by-frame film of my life in sequential order.

The color green continues to be the "magic" bush where my spirit alights during moments of raw emotions, brainstorms and sensations that haven't yet learned to be spoken or written, yet to evolve into story or verse. It is still the color that most often comes to mind as I open my eyes to painful or happy dawns alike. But I must admit that even the greens of memory, at times, march along, treading both my conscious and unconscious streams, in the company of unclassified images and feelings, sounds, textures and smells, names and faces, caresses and tears, sad and happy songs. At others, with the murmur of soft, steady rain or the gales of emotional storms somehow survived. Still, green graces my moments of solitude, reflection and writing.

Sixty years later, as I pedal back over the bumpy roads of my memory, I am fully certain of only one thing: Nineteen fifty-two was and will continue to be one of the most memorable years of my life.

FOUR, FREE AND INVISIBLE

I WAS LUCKY TO SPEND MY FORMATIVE YEARS in a small community that fostered the creation, performance and appreciation of music, dance, poetry and storytelling.

Jáltipan de Morelos, Veracruz, was still a village and had a population of about two thousand the year I was born. A small tropical community on the Gulf of Mexico side of the Isthmus of Tehuantepec, it lay on a tropical savannah about forty minutes by car or cranky bus from the coast. It gained its city status in 1953, after the Azufrera Panamericana—The Pan-American Sulphur Company—began operations there, attracting workers from all over Mexico. The town's population exploded in the next decade. Before then, migration to the southern half of the state trickled down from the Port of Veracruz, where cargo and passenger ships sailing the Atlantic arrived. So it wasn't unusual to find families with North American, German, French and Italian ancestry and surnames, who had arrived from Europe via Cuba and other Caribbean islands where they had relatives and had decided to settle in the region of Sotavento, where Jáltipan was located.

In many of the region's towns, including Jáltipan, four different dialects of the Popoluca were still spoken, in addition to Zapotec and Nahuatl. As expected, Spanish was the dominant language but it still had great competition from Mexicano-Nahuatl, the language of the Mexica people, the Aztecs. My birthplace owes its name to the Nahuatl words for it, Xalti-ipak, which literally means "Place on Sands." During the Post-Conquest era, its name was substituted by its phonetic version in Spanish and became Jáltipan—Hál-tee-pahn.

The old town I called home, until the beginning of 1954, had four major thoroughfares. They fanned out from the main square—*el parque*. Each had an "official" name. Two of them, avenida Morelos and calle Gutiérrez Zamora, respectively led to the Trans-isthmic Highway. At some point, it met the Pan American Highway, which threaded together most of the larger towns throughout Mexico's southeastern states. Calle Morelos was referred to and known by most native Jalti-panecos as "el camino a Cosoleacaque-Minatitlán"—the way to (the towns of) Cosoleacaque-Minatitlan. Calle Gutiérrez Zamora was the way to Acayucan.

If by definition we consider any world community to be multicultural and multilingual when many languages and cultures prosper and benefit from contact with one another, then Jáltipan was such a place. The generations of the Popoluca, the Native Mexicans in the region, were the remaining descendants of the old Olmec, the ancient civilization famous for their carvings of monumental stone heads. When I learned that Popoluca translates into Spanish as "Gente que habla mucho"—People who talk a lot, I found the designation appropriate. Whether inhabitants were pure-blooded descendants of the pre-Columbian Mesoamericans, were mestizos or the offspring of more recent European transplants, the native Jaltipanecos were gregarious. They loved socializing, playing music, singing and dancing, writing and performing poetry, and telling stories.

In most areas of town, we enjoyed the use of electricity, but we lacked other modern conveniences. For example, until I was almost six years old, there was no tap water. People caught rainfall in large drums for washing and bathing. Folks who could afford it paid water carriers to bring cans of drinking water to their doorsteps from the natural springs outside town. Twice a week, Tirso el Aguador—the water carrier—brought the spring water to our home. Sometimes Tirso would let my brother Víctor and me sit on his mules while he emptied the cans into the large drinking water *ollas* in the kitchen.

Water carriers were famous for being among the toughest and most foul-tongued men in the region. Our Tirso was no exception, but unlike other water carriers, he delighted in teaching the children in town some of his favorite colorful expressions and instructed us on the right situation for their use. His lessons began with the simplest and more acceptable words, like *carajo*—darn! or *Qué carajo pasa*—what the heck's (or hell's) going on, for any kind of mistake or minor mishap. Then he moved on to the brighter-redder biggies, which were the more dramatic, hurtful and socially censored expletives involving mothers and other acts, which I, being four years old, could not even begin to grasp. Tirso's tone grew deeper and his gestures became more theatrical as Víctor and I mastered each word in the litany of "biggies" he taught us.

Six and four years old, Víctor and I were Tirso's star pupils. Being a great deal more cautious than I, Víctor did not use this kind of colorful language in front of our parents, and he suggested I follow his example, a warning that I naturally didn't heed. I filled up with those forbidden words, as if they were mangoes or guavas—meaty, sensual and sweet. Encouraged by the soft chuckles of relatives and other adults around me whenever they heard me, I practiced my newly acquired vocabulary often.

While trying to run fast down the stairs to the backyard, I tripped and almost fell down the steps. "¡Ay, chin . . . Casi me mato!"—F..k! I almost killed myself! Busy as I was, rubbing my sore knee, I didn't see my mom until she was standing next to me with a basket of laundry resting on her hip. I covered my mouth with my hand and prayed to everyone in heaven that she hadn't heard me. My throbbing earlobe, pinched between my mom's thumb and index fingernails, made me immediately aware that my plea had gone unheard up there in the celestial kingdom.

Once inside the house, my mother reached for a *chilillo*—a long, skinny, flexible reed—which she kept at hand for those times when we needed to be reminded that when she said no, she meant exactly that. My brother Víctor came running in. When he saw the *chilillo* in my mom's hand, he knew I was going to get it, but he pleaded with my mom, begging her that he, instead of I, be punished. My mom had a soft spot in her heart for Víctor, and my brother had a soft spot in his for me. So my mom whipped the air with the *chilillo*, then put it down, but warned me, "I'll wash your mouth out with soap if I ever hear you use bad language again. That's a promise!"

No question, I was a willful child, and for months I gave her innumerable opportunities to keep her promise . . . and she did. That year, I was the four-year-old with the cleanest, though not necessarily the purest, tongue in town.

Had it not been for the discovery of a recently installed jukebox in a nearby bar, Cantina Cuatro Cañas, I would have literally lost my tongue sooner than later. This electronic contraption, that for twenty Mexican cents, would play anyone's favorite song fascinated me. With five twenty-cent coins—one peso—my brother estimated that we could listen to the same song five consecutive times, a pleasure our old Motorola radio could never provide.

My mother had warned that women—including little girls—were forbidden from going into establishments such as the Cuatro Cañas; terrible things would befall any female who did. So, I did not dare to go inside the bar, but my mother's warning made no mention of boys. It was obvious that young boys were free to run around without T-shirts on very hot days. When there was no bathroom available, they didn't have to hide behind a tree or a car when they peed, or have mom and dad make a shield around them to hide them from the sight of passersby. It then stood to reason—to my four-year-old reason anyway—that boys were again the exception to these rules and that my brother Víctor could safely go into the cantina without any fear of being punished.

At every opportunity, my brother and I asked my mother for twenty cents to buy candy. Then Víctor went into the bar and put the coins in the jukebox. Afterwards, he joined me outside the bar to listen or sing along to "Amorcito Corazón," a ballad sung by the Trío Los Panchos that I particularly enjoyed.

As expected, my mom caught us outside the cantina one day and grounded us for a week. We were to come home directly from school and were not allowed to even play with our friends after doing our homework. To make up for our loss, my father offered to sing our favorite tune to us at bedtime as often as he could. As time went by, he added other ballads to his nightly repertoire. He had a beautiful voice and he could whistle any tune near perfection. His taste in music was eclectic. So, over the next few weeks, Italian songs and French ballads translated and sung in Spanish, as well as Spanish ballads and *pasodobles*—bullfight songs—tropical tunes, Argentine tangos, Mexican *rancheras*, *corridos* and romantic songs, Peruvian and Mexican waltzes, Caribbean rhythms and *boleros tropicales*, and many other types of music, found their way to my bedside, weaving the fabric of dreams with threads of woe and joy in lands faraway. When I was older, I began to fantasize about the day I too could be consumed by my love for a matador in Madrid or Sevilla, or in some other exotic land, lose my heart to a wild and passionate man.

In some haphazard and odd ways, some of the romantic dreams I had then have been partially fulfilled. When I was twelve, while listening to his life story on the radio, I fell in love with the Spanish matador Manuel Rodríguez, "Manolete," who died a year after I was born; however, I did not set foot in Spain until I was thirty-five years old and spent three days in Barcelona on my way to Italy, then pursued my destiny in Austria and Germany. Although I have never been to Lima or Buenos Aires, in the '70s I lost a chunk of my heart and suffered the slings and arrows of political and romantic misfortune in that "farout," exotic land called Berkeley, California.

Despite the two-year difference between us, Víctor and I were inseparable. It was 1949, and he had to begin school. Although in time his willingness to have me as a constant companion would change, that late winter, despite promises and threats, Víctor refused to start school without me. The only way any four-year-old could attend school was by permission from the principal and the first-grade teacher.

Whenever people became too nosy about each other's private affairs, my mother was fond of saying that a tiny town can be, and often is, a big hell. There is no way to keep private any wrongdoing or good deed, or retain any kind of anonymity from the rest of the townspeople, but, one of the advantages of living in a "tiny big hell" is precisely that people know one another well. In my case, this proved to be a blessing since my parents knew *Profesor* Martínez, the school principal, well. My father took Víctor and me to see him.

"Víctor refuses to come to school without his sister," my father explained. "Would it be all right if she comes with him?" he asked, then reassured his friend, "Just for a while?"

"I'll talk to Víctor's teacher and explain. I'm sure she'll agree, as long as your daughter is quiet and stays out of the way," the principal said. "As a matter of fact, we can put an extra desk for her in the back of the room. But keep in mind that, even if she stays the whole year, she will have to start the first grade when she finally reaches the legal age to attend."

"Understood," my father replied.

Once Víctor and I knew that we would be able to attend school together, we wandered around the building and grounds while the adults finished their conversation. Parents of schoolage children, my father among them, had headed the fundraising efforts to build this new school. Proudly, everyone pointed out that, unlike the old school, this new site had a separate classroom for each grade.

I liked the new school's shiny tile floors and the smell of fresh paint, but I had also liked the old school in the Pulido sisters' house and backyard, where for years children six to twelve had received individualized and group instruction. Sometimes, on hot days, instruction took place outdoors, under the canopy of two enormous mango trees. I had been to that outdoor school one time with my mother. I was fascinated, for the mango trees were also home to a family of parrots the Pulido sisters had not been able to chase away.

In those days, the academic year ran from February to early December. The birds were gone most of the day, except during the mango season—May, June and July—when they were joined by their feathered relatives and friends to feast at home. The parrots provided an alternate chorus to the children's daily recitations, driving the sisters to the brink of hysteria. The Pulido School began to lose some of its students after the opening of the new public school, the primary school Víctor and I were now sure we would attend.

Two days after my father talked to the principal, Víctor and I began school. As told, I was given a desk in the back of the classroom. I liked sitting in a corner, with a commanding view of the room, intrigued and amused by all the goings-on inside, and thoroughly fascinated with the subjects we studied. During the next two-hundred school days, I sat in my little corner quietly content. Quietly also, I learned to read and write, to add and subtract, to tell fruit from flower, clock from calendar, caterpillar from worm, dolphin from shark.

Only months earlier, my tongue had eagerly enjoyed the ripeness and texture of forbidden words. Now, like a first child in paradise, my mouth filled with the names of animals and plants that flourished in faraway lands, as I learned about the ethereal grace of epiphytic orchids, the majestic but awesome presence of tigers in the nights of the planet, and the power of the collective in the works of bees. I also began to pay more attention to my own tropical world.

"They're beautiful, aren't they?" *Profesor* Martínez said one time he found me looking at a book on insects. "The world really belongs to you, the children, and to the insects," he added.

At an intuitive level, I understood what he meant, for I had already been aware of the work of army ants and had witnessed the birth of many butterflies. I had followed the luminous paths of myriad fireflies soaring a few feet from the ground, like a restless reflection of the Milky Way. I had heard the song of the cicadas all day long and the chorus of crickets in the evening that provided background music to my grandmother's tales of buried treasures and the ghosts who guarded them.

Sitting in the back corner of the classroom, I also glimpsed the terrible suffering people can inflict on one another, as I watched one of my classmates, a girl who had befriended me, grow more depressed each day. The bruises on her arms got larger, darker, more frequent and painful to my touch. One day, she did not come back to school. I cried when my mother told me that my classmate was dead.

Although my first academic year ended on such a sad note, I was looking forward to the end-of-the-year festivities. Naively, I asked if I could participate in the cultural program or if my drawings could be included in the students' art exhibit, but I was refused. Everyone liked me, and the teachers admired my tenacity and constancy, but I wasn't even a name or a file number on the school roster. I was four, free to go to school or stay home, but I was also an illegal student. I was invisible. The next year, nonetheless, no one objected to my returning to school. So my brother and I started the second grade. At the end of that second year, everyone was pleased that I would be legally attending school the following February.

For two years, my father had been correcting and helping me with my homework. More than anyone else, he knew how well I had learned first- and second-grade subjects, so my dad asked the principal to let me go on to the third grade instead, and he agreed. After obtaining consensus from the faculty, he wrote to the state department of education asking for an exception in my case.

Like most government offices in the world, the department was notoriously slow, so the principal was surprised, unpleasantly, when he received a prompt reply. What was he thinking? Not only was his request for my promotion to the third grade denied, but he was also admonished for allowing a four-year-old to attend primary school.

Trying to remain calm, my father informed me that I had to repeat the first and second grades. I suppose he expected me to be upset about it, but when I showed no displeasure, he was intrigued.

"Doesn't this make you unhappy?" he asked.

"No," I replied. "It's all right. I can work on the projects I couldn't do when I was going with Víctor."

"Won't that be boring for you?"

"No," I reassured him. However, my father looked disappointed, so I hastily added, "But I'll go to the third grade if you want me to."

He laughed. A week later, however, he started his own campaign, aided by *Profesor* Martínez and backed by six teachers, the school's custodian and some other parents in favor of my promotion. Very soon, my defense committee—small but determined—was waging epistolary and telegraphic war against the state department of education.

Two weeks before school started, the principal received word that I was to take the final exams for all subjects in the first and second grades. According to my dad, if I passed them with ninety percent accuracy, they would consider placing me in the second grade, but never (!) in the third grade. I was too young and, if that weren't enough, granting the request would set an undesirable precedent. Everyone, including the teachers, complained about the unfairness of the decision, but the department's attitude was one of take-it-or-leave-it. Since there seemed to be no choice, I was given the tests, which I passed with only an occasional mistake.

On the first school day in February 1951, my father and I walked into the second-grade classroom. My teacher showed me to a student desk in the front row, close to her desk, but I wasn't happy there. She allowed me to sit at my usual place in the remote corner of the room. Because I already knew the subjects well, I was often asked to tutor other students.

The following year, trying to keep me challenged, my third-grade teacher, *Profesora* Diana, began to instruct me in the recitation of poetry. She taught me how to deliver an impeccable line by sensing the rhythm of the poem, in the same way that my piano teacher later helped me to understand musical phrasing. She also showed me how to breathe so a full line would be delivered uninterrupted, and how to use voice modulation and gestures to keep the poem alive for the listener.

When she felt satisfied with my rhetorical skills, she asked me to memorize patriotic poems. Standing on a stepping stool, I recited them before an audience during national holidays. My father was thrilled to have me perform, but he objected to my learning only patriotic poems. So he asked my teacher to expose me to other kinds of poetry. I memorized, then recited in public López Velarde's "Suave Patria" and many other age-appropriate poems by Mexican and Latin American poets, especially those written by the Nicaraguan Rubén Darío and the Chilean Gabriela Mistral.

During the school's celebration of Mother's Day that year, I recited a poem about a young boy whose mother had died. Afraid that people would notice my trembling hands, I kept them laced on my chest and concentrated on delivering my lines correctly. Little by little, I began to experience the intensity of the feelings in the poem, to appropriate the pain of that orphan boy as if I myself had lost my mother.

At some point, I was aware of the unusual silence in the audience. Perhaps they were not enjoying the poem because I wasn't using hand gestures to keep the poem "alive" for them. Still, I kept my hands laced over my chest until I delivered the last line. Then, I really looked at people. They were staring at me with teary eyes. Suddenly, they began to clap hard then harder. Overwhelmed by the audience's enthusiastic response and the intense feelings in the poem, I ran to my father and took refuge in his arms. Twenty-five years later, already living in California, and writing poems of my own, I would revisit that childhood memory at a poetry reading three thousand miles away from my hometown.

During and after the Chicano Movement in the 1970s, I was asked many times to share my poems with an audience at Floricanto Festivals—*flor*-poem, *canto*-song—where many Chicano/a poets and musicians performed their work. At one of those events, I was invited by the celebrated Chicano bilingual poet José Montoya to read at the Reno Club in Sacramento. José, like his brother Malaquías Montoya a renowned Chicano painter and master print-maker, championed the idea that poetry, visual arts and music should be available to our communities at a variety of venues, outside the walls and halls of academia. The Reno Club was a place where people gathered to celebrate Chicano culture, listen to music, sing and dance, and poetry fit perfectly among the other performing cultural arts. As a child, I had listened to music outside a cantina, but I had never read in a bar or nightclub before, and accepted the invitation with a bit of trepidation. A bar was a noisy, busy place. What if people didn't like my reading or my poetry and went on talking and carrying on, or booed me off the stage? Somehow, my child's ego hadn't been as insecure as the grown woman's was by then. I would muster up the courage somehow, I promised myself.

My dear friends, Alcides and Catherine Rodríguez-Nieto, had driven up from the Bay Area with me. Catherine had translated into English the poems I was reading that night and was looking forward to hearing me read, since I had planned to read mine in Spanish, followed by her translations. At the door, we were given the program, and I was the first poet to read.

That night, Ricardo Sánchez, a well-known Chicano poet from Texas, had joined the group of performers uninvited and unannounced. Had he simply wanted to read his poetry, there would have been no problem, but when I asked, someone told me Ricardo wanted to show a film, and José Montoya tried to point out that the program had been finalized and there were many poets reading that night. Ricardo had made no previous arrangements, but he insisted, and arguments went up a few decibels and back and forth when others joined in the tug-of-war. I had been talking with poets Francisco X. Alarcón and Juan Felipe Herrera, whom I had met for the first time and who were also scheduled to read that night, when a visibly frustrated José approached us and said, "Okay, let's get started. Lucha, you're on!"

I went up the steps to the stage, trying not to hear the loud voices, the insults going back and forth, not to see the fists in the air, the open hands reaching for the film to tear it apart, all a short distance from me. I took a sweeping look at the room, saw customers at the bar waiting for their drinks and heard the loud clinks and clangs of bottles, glasses and metal as the bartenders filled orders. I fixed my eyes on the mirror above the bar for a brief moment, hoped for the best, raised my reading material to eye level and got closer to the mike. My memory is fuzzy and I barely remember explaining that I would read my poems in Spanish first, then Catherine's English translation, or something to that effect. I took a deep breath, tried my best to tune out the din, and began to read in Spanish, slowly at first. Then the spirit of the poem swirled in my chest and took possession of my voice.

At some point, I looked up and realized that the bartenders had stopped serving drinks and that people in the audience, including Ricardo and warring foes, had quieted down. When I finished my reading, for an instant the silence seemed overwhelming. After a quick "thank you," I walked to the steps. Then people began to clap harder and harder. My eyes slid over the many unknown, yet friendly and smiling faces. I was suddenly aware that I was looking for my late father's countenance among them, but this time he wasn't there to hold me in his arms, as he had twenty-seven years earlier when I'd recited the poem about the orphan boy. My orphaned heart beat like a distant drum inside me. Its rhythms were the cadences of Spanish—my father's language, the language of my music and forever the language of my poetry. It was the reverence for that language that the audience in the Reno Club and I shared that night, thirty-some years ago.

Ricardo Sánchez's path and mine would cross again a few years later in San Antonio. I had been invited by Sandra Cisneros to teach a two-week summer poetry workshop at the Guadalupe Cultural Arts Center. Sandra had just resigned as the center's coordinator of the literature program and was already gone for the summer. I knew no one there. The center had asked someone to look after my needs, and she had to the extent she could. I hadn't met either the director of the center or any of the other staff. So I was pretty much on my own, with the exception of the late poet and activist Angela de Hoyos and her husband Moisés, who immediately adopted me and I them, and who, together with the poets in my workshop, saw to my comfort in any and all ways open to them. Angela was indeed a wonderful woman and poet and my guardian angel while I was there.

Part of my program at the Guadalupe Center was to give a public reading of my poetry. I was warned that Ricardo Sánchez wanted to interview me and to publicize the reading in the local newspaper. He had a reputation of being a very difficult man and a tough interviewer, especially as it concerned poets' cultural and political credentials as Chicanos/as.

I was given the option of not accepting, but I was also told it would be great promotion for the reading if the interview was a success.

"Don't pretend to be what you aren't. Live your life by what you dearly believe in. No pretexts. No regrets." My grandmother Nico's words of advice struck one another like billiard balls and rolled into the pockets of my mind, as I saw Ricardo waiting for me at the café where we were meeting. Interestingly enough, we spent three hours together and exchanged stories about the movement, poetry, San Antonio vis-a-vis San Francisco Bay Area, California and Texas, classical and Mexican music and my story as an immigrant. He then invited me to visit his bookstore and meet other local poets he hosted there every Sunday afternoon, and I attended the next gathering of poets. Yet, not even in passing did he refer to the fracas at the Floricanto poetry reading at Sacramento's Reno Club—by then known as "The Last Canto"—that had left him with a bruised face and ego and with a film strewn all over the floor. Nor did he ever mention seeing or hearing me read at the club, and I respected his reasons for the omission.

The day before my public presentation in San Antonio, Angela came to the workshop as usual. In hand, she had the local newspaper opened to Ricardo's interview of me. He had given me and my poetry a glowing review, his seal of approval, and was urging San Antonians to attend my reading and ask plenty during the Q and A following the reading. We had an excellent showing.

When asked if my poems spoke to my own experience, I only answered with generalities, to say, for example, that my own life experience is but the platform the poem uses to take flight and reach that place where we all share in our humanity and humaneness as Mexicans, Americans, and as people. I talk about being a lyrical poet, that I hardly write narrative poetry. When I am asked why, I explain that I come from a very strong Mexican and Latin American literary tradition that gives great importance to lyrical poetry, that in the United States, narrative poetry is valued above all others. I argue for acceptance of both traditions as equal anywhere in the world.

Regardless of the importance we give to one kind of poetry over another, in the end the only important truth is that words have the power to communicate the ineffable and to help us transcend our individual lives. Like every other poet before and after me, I am the language power broker.

Although so far I have fearlessly protected my right to write about anything and in any poetic voice I please, I do admit that every time I decide to submit any poem or story for publication, I stop at the open mouth of the mailbox, and for an instant I consider what it will cost me to bare my soul in public. I usually drop the envelope in the box. I hear it hit bottom, and I get on my way, remembering the deceptively sweet but caustic sensation of soap on my tongue—the price I once paid for the use of such power.

EPIPHANY: THE THIRD GIFT

EVER SINCE I WAS FOUR YEARS OLD, women insisted on giving me dolls. By age seven, I had an assortment of them, made of papier-mâché, clay and cloth. My grandmother Nicolasa had also made a few of them for me out of my older cousin's stockings. One of my mother's friends had brought me a porcelain "little lady" from Mexico City, which was kept in my mother's wardrobe so I wouldn't break or damage it in any way.

As a child, I didn't understand why everyone around me insisted on giving me dolls, especially since I had made it clear that I really didn't like playing with them. I much more enjoyed climbing trees and running around with the boys— my older brother, a cousin and their friends. I loved playing marbles, spinning tops till they hummed. Walking the high wire on a narrow brick fence or swinging like Tarzan on long vines from a tree were some of our favorite activities. Most of all, I preferred reading. During recess and after school, I would go into an area in the principal's office that doubled as the school library. I would look at the illustrations and read over and over the few natural science and biology books kept on a table there. At home, after doing my homework, I would consume any text lying around.

At the time, my father, who worked for the Mexican National Telegraph Company, had undergone a cornea transplant and had to wear a patch over one of his eyes. Straining his other eye, he slowly read the daily reports coming into his office, but by the time he went home, that eye was burning. After supper, he would ask me to read to him selections from the regional and national newspapers. I was happy to do something for my father, whom I loved very much, but reading to him also gave me an opportunity to learn new words. He would patiently explain anything I didn't understand. Although I didn't fully grasp the issues reported in the news articles, I did begin to learn about international, national and regional politics, geography, poetry and folklore.

Reading and looking at my small tropical world from high above the tallest trees became more exciting than playing with those cute celluloid creatures that could do nothing but stare into empty space. Every so often I'd rub my face against the silky surface of the cloth dolls, feel the warm terseness of the papier-mâché under my fingers or the smooth coolness of the porcelain, whenever my mother allowed me to hold the doll in her wardrobe. To my mother's chagrin, however, most of the time the dolls rested one upon the other like fallen dominoes alongside a wall in my room.

For a few months after my sixth birthday, no one—including my mother—had given me any dolls, and I thought the adults around me had finally gotten over their need to do so, but I was wrong, for the sixth of January neared. Like millions of children in Mexico, at home, we received presents on the Twelfth Night after the birth of Jesus Christ—Epiphany—a time to commemorate the revealing of baby Jesus to the Magi and their offering to him of myrrh, incense and gold.

On that January 6, 1952, my parents gave me three gifts: a doll (no great surprise!), a doll's house and a book—a children's version of *One Thousand and One Arabian Nights*, which came wrapped in red tissue paper. I used the wrapping tissue as a book cover and was just getting ready to read when my mother walked into my room.

"Isn't your doll just beautiful?" my mother asked.

I looked at the doll (I'll call her *She* because I never gave her a name). *She* was a fair celluloid creature with light brown hair and blue eyes that matched the color of her ruffled dress. Her apron and socks were white. I puckered my lips and raised my eyebrows, not really knowing how to let my mother down easily.

"But this one is different," my mother explained, trying to talk me into playing with the toy. "Look. This doll talks; she says, 'Mommy.'" Then she turned the doll over, raised her tiny dress and pulled on a chain to wind the doll's voice mechanism, but something must have been wrong with it because the noises *She* made sounded more like a cat's cries than a baby's babble.

My grandmother had often told me that our neighbor's cat cried like that because it needed love. "*Anda buscando amor*— it's looking for love," she explained, purposely neglecting to elaborate on the kind of love a cat in heat desires.

Interpreting my grandmother's comment literally, on several occasions I had tried to hug the cat to give it love, but it had scratched me and run away. Sure, that the doll needed love, I hugged her tightly for a long time. Useless, I said to myself finally as the doll kept making the cat-looking-for-love noises. I decided to play instead with the doll's house, which my father had set down on the front porch, where it was cooler in the late afternoon. I went to play with it, but because inspecting and rearranging the tiny furniture seemed to be the only activity possible, I quickly lost interest.

I could hear my friends in the yard talking and egging each other on to walk the high wire. Bending over or squatting to play with the doll's house had left my body and spirit in need of a good stretch, so I went into my room to put on my shoes to join my friends in the yard. I was tying my shoelaces when I saw again the third of my gifts, *One Thousand and One Arabian Nights*, wrapped in red tissue paper, and I began to read it. From that moment on, the doll and the doll's house began to collect dust, and Scheherazade became my constant companion.

Every day after doing my homework, I climbed the guava tree in our yard. Nestled among its branches during the next few weeks, I read and reread the Scheherazade's stories to my heart's content. I was unaware that my mother had become concerned because I wasn't playing with either the doll or the little house.

My parents had always encouraged us to read. My mother wouldn't have dreamed of asking me to give up my time reading, but she began to insist that I take the doll up the tree with me.

Trying to read on a branch fifteen feet above ground while holding onto the silly doll was not an easy feat. Not even for an *artist of the high wire and the flying trapeze*. After nearly falling off the branch twice, I finally had to devise a way to please my mother but keep my neck intact. Cutting two thin vines off a tree, I removed the skin and tied them together into one long rope; then I tied one end around the doll's neck and the opposite one around the branch. This way I could just let the doll hang in midair while I read.

I was looking out for my mother, though. I sensed that my playing with the doll was of great importance to her. So every time I heard my mother coming, I lifted the doll up and hugged her. The smile in my mother's eyes told me my plan was working. Before suppertime, I entered the house through the kitchen so my mother could see me holding the doll.

For the next few days, my mother, the doll and I were quite happy, but the inevitable happened one afternoon. Totally absorbed in the reading, I did not hear my mother calling me until she was right under the tree. When I looked down, I saw my mother, her mouth open in disbelief, staring at the dangling doll. Fearing the worst, I climbed down in a flash, reaching the ground just as my mother was untying the doll.

"And what is *this?*" she asked, as she smoothed out the doll's dress.

My mother always asked that when she wanted me to admit to some wrongdoing. From that point on, we would follow an unwritten script. After my giving the appropriate answer for the particular situation we faced, "It's a doll hanging," in this case—my mother would then ask me a second question, like, "And why is this doll hanging from the tree?"

To my surprise, however, on this occasion my mother wasn't following the script. Dumbfounded, she kept on staring at the doll then glanced at me. I swallowed hard, as I realized that I had just accomplished the impossible: I had rendered my mother speechless! I also sensed for the first time in my seven years that I had done something terribly, terribly wrong, perhaps even unforgivable.

Making me carry the doll in my arms, my mother led me back to the house, still without a reprimand, but I was sure that I would be paying for my transgression by nightfall when my father came home. By suppertime, I feared, the storm would hover right above my head, but my father came home, and supper came and went, and I went to bed at my usual time with my ears, hands and butt untouched.

The day after the hanging-doll incident, my father came home early and suggested that he and I play with the doll's house. He had stopped by my grandmother's house a block away and had picked up some tiny clay bowls, cups and pots she had bought for me. Among the kitchenware there was even a tiny *metate*, in case we wanted to grind the *nixtamal*— lye-softened corn—to make tortillas, he said.

Dust had already collected on the roof of the little house and on the tiny furniture. It took us awhile to wipe everything clean before we could begin to put all the furnishings back in the rooms.

When everything was finally ready, I realized that playing with the doll's house this second time was just as boring as the first, but my father seemed to be having so much fun that I didn't have the heart to tell him I wasn't in the least interested. So quietly I slipped back into my room and picked up Scheherazade on my way to the yard. Absorbed as he was in arranging and rearranging the tiny furniture, he didn't even take notice of my quick exit.

At suppertime, again, I expected a good earlobe pinching. Instead, waving a finger but laughing, my father said, "Ah, *mi chaparrita traviesa*—my naughty little girl."

"Miguel Ángel, you're spoiling this child," my mother objected.

My father's only reply was a chuckle.

Almost twenty years passed before I found out from both my parents why the hanging-doll episode had been so significant for them. By then I was twenty-six, had already been living in Berkeley since 1964, my father had already been diagnosed with terminal cancer, and I was a parent myself.

After recounting the episode of the hanging doll amid my dad's and my laughter, my mother got teary-eyed and sentimental. She confessed that all those years she had been afraid I would turn out to be an unnatural mother because, as a child, I had hung the doll from the branch. She was delighted I had turned out to be a loving and understanding mother to my then four-year-old son, Arturo.

During my nineteen years at home, neither my father nor my mother ever gave up trying to socialize me—"civilize me," my mother would often say. They always affirmed that I was as intellectually and artistically capable as my brothers. And they provided me with the best education they could afford. They made clear to me, nonetheless, that all this was being done not just to satisfy my own needs as an individual. Above all, I was being educated to serve the needs of the family I'd one day have.

"When you educate a man, you educate an individual. But when you educate a woman, you educate the whole family," my father would often tell my younger sister Conchita and me. Lightly caressing my sister's cheek then mine, he'd add, "I don't remember who said that a child's education begins twenty years before he or she is born. But whoever said it was surely right. My grandchildren's education begins with yours, my little women."

It wasn't unusual for Mexican fathers, almost regardless of class, to deny their daughters the advantages of formal schooling on the false premise that as women they would always be supported and protected by their husbands, and in the worst case by their brothers. Besides, even if a woman learned a profession, she would not be able to make a career of it, because she would end up staying at home to take care of the family. In view of that, educating a woman was just a waste of time. The important thing was then to get a husband as successful as could be found for the girls in the family. "Problem solved," some of my uncles and other male parents in town perfunctorily stated.

My father was not quite the typical Mexican father in this respect, but even this atypical man, who has been and will continue to be one of the most influential people in my life, was subject to the social norms and pressures that made the education of a woman a separate (if equal) experience. Consistently throughout my life at home, I was convinced by both my parents that what I truly wanted, a career in medicine, was not what was best for me.

"As a medical doctor you'll have to care for and examine male patients—you'll be subject to men's low designs," my father warned.

"And you will suffer," my mother added, waving her finger admonishingly to emphasize what she really wanted to say: "Conform!"

With impeccable logic, my father would state the advantages of a career in dentistry for a woman: independence (not working for a man), flexibility of schedule (time to take care of a family as well) and great financial rewards (in case I became a widow and sole supporter of the family).

Seen from his point of view it all made sense, but I could not see myself as a dentist. Relentlessly, I would then plead for a career in astronomy. My father would caress my cheek gently and say, "But, my little woman, an astronomer has to work at night. When would you spend time with your children? And your husband, surely he would find someone else to keep him company at night."

"And you will suffer," my mother would interject in her usual manner. "Your children will grow up having a zombie for a mother, and you'll die young," she would add with a stern face, as if I were already the victim of an ancient curse.

Because I wanted to pursue a career, I eventually agreed to attend the school of dentistry in San Luis Potosí, where we had moved when I was eight years old and where I received most of my formal education. I was happy the first two years in dentistry, because I carried the same subjects as medical students, in addition to dental labs. But when I stared into a real open mouth for the first time, I began to suspect that I was not cut out to be a good dentist. The first time I sweated out the extraction of a molar, my suspicions were confirmed. And I knew I would surely go insane or drive that dental drill past the pulp and the roots of a tooth all the way to a patient's throat one day, and spend the rest of my life in prison. Hoping and praying that I would learn to like being a dentist, but mostly to please my father, I agreed to stay in dentistry school. Mercifully, life had other plans for me.

Since I was sixteen years old, I had been going steady with Guillermo Hernández, who was preparing to move to Berkeley, where he intended to get his B.A. from the University of California. As painful as it was to leave my family and my country, I had no qualms in quitting dentistry, marrying him and moving to California. Through my relationship with my husband and his own interests in literature and philosophy, I rediscovered reading for my own enjoyment and personal growth. Although I would not start writing poetry for another five years after my arrival in Berkeley, I knew I wanted to make the study of literature my life's pursuit.

By the time I began writing poetry, I was already undergoing a painful separation from my husband, feeling cut off from the cultural and emotional support of family and friends, working as a bilingual secretary to support my son and put myself through college at U.C. Berkeley, grieving for my late father and expressing my daily thoughts and experiences in a language not yet my own.

For the next few years, in an almost manic manner, I wrote at least one poem a day, possessed by the terrifying notion that if I stopped writing I would stop breathing as well.

From time to time, during my visits with my mother in San Luis Potosí, she would recall the incident of the hanging doll and thank God aloud for making me a good parent. Then she'd sigh as she inventoried my vicissitudes in life, pointing out that I would be a rich dentist and a happily married woman still living in Mexico, instead of being a divorcée and single mother, a poor schoolteacher and Chicana poet in California.

I often look back at that same childhood incident, recall my third gift, the book I wrapped in red tissue paper, and for a fleeting instant I, too, take inventory of the experiences that have made me who and what I am. I pause to marvel at life's wondrous ironies.

LA PÁGINA ROJA

SINCE I STARTED SCHOOL AT AGE FOUR, by age six I could read well enough. My father asked that I read the daily news to him to keep my skills up. At the time, the national and the regional newspapers had a separate crime page—*la página roja*. It was a loose sheet so parents could easily remove it to keep children from reading it. My father let me select readings from any page, except of course *la página roja*. He dutifully removed it, folded it and put it in his shirt pocket to dispose of it later. Since there was no threat of punishment, I was not deterred from finding the red page at every opportunity and reading all about accidents, murders, brawls in the *zona roja* (red light district), white slavery and gambling. Although I didn't know exactly what prostitution and gambling were all about, I guessed they were serious social and moral offenses but not necessarily illegal. The sale of minors or adult women to houses of ill-repute and the use of human beings in a wager, however, were felonies as grave as homicide.

My grandfather had gambled away some of his property in card games. Not surprisingly, we were all lectured on the evils of gaming. Ironically, every week, my father played the national lottery. The nuances in criminal law and my father's own behavior eluded my grasp back then, but I suspected that prostitution and gambling were among "the sins of the flesh" the town priest cautioned everyone against, pointing his index finger to the sky. "But you must ward off the sins of the mind for they are indeed more insidious than the sins of the flesh," he admonished.

"More than anyone, he surely knows the flesh is weak," my grandmother used to tell my aunt. To me, she would say, "Don't let any man, including the priest, get to that little turtle between your legs." But I was more concerned with my sins. I was not only disobeying my father by reading (*La página roja*) the red page, I was also committing "an insidious sin of the mind." I would say a few Hail Marys just in case and make a mental note to ask the priest about the meaning of it all on my first confession in a year. Waiting for clarification, I continued enjoying the red page but began to tire of reading about brawls, brothels, knifings, shootings and accidents in all gory but repetitive details. Instead, I became intrigued by crimes that involved duplicity and premeditation—"intelligence," such as the case of a woman married to an abusive, lecherous man—Ema and Luis for the purpose of the story, Desperate, Ema attempted to poison Luis by mixing in his *huevos rancheros* a large amount of a toxic powder she made of ground cashew nut shells. Ema was an amateur murderer and left a trail of clues for the *gendarmes* investigating the case. Evidence piled against her.

One night, the men were at the square talking and singing. The women in the family and other friends sat in the breezeway, as they did sometimes after supper. Some of them offered their opinion about Ema's case, and I got my first lessons on how to commit the perfect crime.

"Lesson one: Be as far away from him as possible when he ingests the poison. And for God's sake, resist the sweet desire to watch him squirm!"

"Lesson two: She just didn't know how to do it right. She should have put the deadliest of coral snakes in his underwear drawer. He reaches for his *calzones* and ZAS, he's history. After all, those snakes wander into houses and their poison is quick and lethal."

"Lesson three: Maybe she wanted to be caught."

"But maybe she reached her limit and was desperate enough."

"No. She knew what she was doing. The sad part is that Luis didn't die, but the poison left him insane."

"Huh! The poison didn't make him go crazy. Terror did. A warning to abusive and lecherous husbands, *sí, señor*."

"I just don't believe that he's truly insane."

The women agreed.

I never heard my father or the men comment on that or any other case, but I didn't dare ask for my dad's opinion about this or any other murder, lest I confess reading *la página roja*.

Whether the almost-murdered man was mad or not, there was no trial. The judge simply sentenced Ema to take care of her invalid husband for life. Her hometown became her prison, townsfolk her guards watching her every move. Ema would never be able to make another attempt on her husband's life, never be free of him. No one was surprised when this unrepentant wife hanged herself from a beam in her living room. About a year later, I read a social note in the papers. Luis had made a miraculous recovery and was about to marry a wealthy widow in a neighboring port city. Weeks after he married the rich widow, *la página roja* reported that he had been arrested for beating a prostitute to death.

After supper that evening, my mother joined my grandmother in the breezeway. My grandmother sat in her favorite chair with me on her lap. No one was eager to talk. Then unexpectedly my mother said, "He'll probably get off, free. Not a day in jail. Money talks."

"Lesson four: Tell me, who's the real criminal? Not her," my grandmother said. "There is no justice in this world."

As I rested my head on my grandmother's chest, all I could hear was her heart pounding against flesh and bone.

My grandmother died when I was nineteen, two months after I got married and moved to Berkeley, five years before I started writing poems, ten before I began to write stories and thirty-three before I wrote *Black Widow's Wardrobe*, the story of a woman who, in 1972, kills her abusive husband.

Licia, the "Black Widow" in my novel, is the victim of her abusive husband. She kills him. Extenuating circumstances or not, her own sense of justice demands that she be punished. The legal system agrees with her, but it stacks the deck against her as it did against Ema. Unlike Ema, Licia is legally tried but by an all-male jury. Convicted, she is sentenced to eighteen years in prison. Upon her release, someone tries to kill her and Chicana detective Gloria Damasco is hired to find out who and why.

During the investigation, Gloria begins to explore the nature of justice. How absolute a notion is it in the face of discrimination, abuse or the sociopolitical reality encountered by people—particularly women—of color in the system? How do law and justice interact with or prey upon each other? Is true justice really attainable by all? What role does compassion play in the administering of justice?

In my novel, *Eulogy for a Brown Angel*, Gloria Damasco, as a woman of color and a political activist, seeks answers to those questions. She finds a young child dead during the 1970 National Chicano Moratorium protest march and riot in Los Angeles. Gloria suspects that a Chicano journalist is responsible for the murder of both the child and a young gang member, a possible witness to the deed. L.A. Homicide Detective Kenyon asks for her help to entrap the suspected Chicano journalist. For the L.A. detective things are simple, and he takes his personal and moral concerns for granted, because in the solution of a crime, justice is served and goodness prevails. For Gloria, there is more at stake than restoring the order upset by the murders. In her words:

"In the summer of 1970, everything anyone of us did had to be considered according to its political impact on the Chicano community. So . . . I supported the unwritten rule that forbade Chicanos to go public on any issues that could be used to justify discrimination against us. . . . I treaded on a quagmire of the conscience . . . accepted as (my) right and responsibility the function of making sure that justice was dealt equally to everyone. . . . But goodness, like justice, was only a relative notion, depending on who interpreted or administered it. . . . "

Gloria grapples with her conscience, considers dropping the investigation altogether. If she serves as bait for the killer, a Chicano, she will become an outcast in her community, never to be trusted again. But letting the murderer of an innocent child go free is heavier in her conscience. The scales have been tipped. She needs to understand the forces that would compel someone to take the life of a child. As Gloria poses the question to me, I also wrestle with my own prejudices and concept of justice. The murderer must pay, I tell her. But my detective isn't satisfied.

For a day, sleep-deprived, I sit in front of the computer unable to write as my detective refuses to go on with the story. Still, I wonder why she is so bent on exploring the murderer's point of view, his own experience as a blue-eyed blond child who unfoundedly feels rejected by his own mother in favor of the older dark-skinned son, and the kind of rage that motivates him not to kill his brother but his brother's child. My eyes hurt badly. I close them for a moment and fall asleep, but my heart starts to race. I am breathing through my mouth. And I instinctively open my eyes. "It's so simple," I tell Gloria. "Love is compassion. A mother accepts that her child has done something terribly wrong and he must pay for his deeds. But she still loves him. Why else would a mother visit her son in prison, even when everyone tells her she shouldn't, that he's a monster?"

Then, I really open my eyes. I have just had a dream within a dream. Or is it an epiphany? Dream or epiphany—it matters little as Gloria, satisfied with my answer, takes over again, and I resume my writing. Eventually, I came to realizations of great personal value to me, as a woman and a writer:

1) Justice is a living organism, mutating, evolving. Like a poem, it takes substance and form from incongruent elements at various levels of consciousness and the subconscious. Both poetry and justice, however, are elusive. They both require from us that we stop and listen—acknowledge.

2) Our sense of justice also requires that we act on the knowledge, that we calibrate our conscience with compassion and empathy, for without them true justice is not possible.

3) For me, as a Chicana mystery writer, acting on that knowledge means writing.

Although the mystery story falls under the category of "popular fiction," writing it is not as easy as it seems. Since the publication of Edgar Allan Poe's *The Purloined Letter*, the detective story has changed little. It is a plot-driven long or short story, leaving room for little more than the solution of the crime. The challenge—the art—for any crime writer rests in finding ways to offer much more than the unraveling of the plot, bringing to justice those who have broken the law and restoring the social order.

Chicana/Chicano crime fiction may follow some, many or all of the conventions, traditions and structural demands of the genre, but it breaks away from them in the treatment of Chicana/Chicano themes and the development of characters steeped and deeply rooted in the culture. Thematically, our crime novels fit perfectly within Chicana/Chicano literature, exploring themes such as:

- Spirituality, religion and the struggle between good and evil.
- The search for justice and socioeconomic equality, human and civil rights, the history of the Mexican people in Mexico and in the United States and the border and La Migra.
- The cultural and linguistic wealth in the various and distinctive Chicano communities in the Southwest, and the re-interpretation of legend and myth.
- Sexism, homophobia and racism, and other gender and gender-preference issues within the culture and in the larger context of a multicultural United States.

Chicana/Chicano crime fiction offers in some cases the best vehicle to explore many of these subjects in a direct, although sometimes shocking, manner. It reflects the reality of ordinary people, like us, who find themselves in the midst of strife, violence and injustice, to which they have perhaps become oblivious, or that they feel powerless to change. Guided by the detective's moral-ethical compass, crime fiction offers a way to engage emotionally and work through those moral-ethical dilemmas. In the process, our perception of the world about us changes, and the possibility of obtaining justice for ourselves, as for others, becomes a more tenable objective.

Some well-known Latin American male writers have penned at least one mystery novel, perhaps intrigued by the possibilities of sociopolitical commentary offered by the genre, or simply because crafting a detective novel or a thriller is good discipline for any writer. But the fact is that in Latin American as in Spanish literature the noir novel, until recently, has been the exception—an oddity.

In Mexico, decades before Paco Ignacio Taibo II began to gain recognition for his very popular detective fiction series and made the writing of crime fiction legitimate, Luis Spota had the dubious honor of being the only Mexican crime fiction writer. In Cuba as in Spain the number of crime fiction writers has quadrupled in the last decade. For the most part, the writers of crime fiction in these countries are men. Such is the case of Chicano/Chicana crime fiction.

In 1984, Rolando Hinojosa's *Partners in Crime* was published as part of his series, *Klail City Death Trips*. Rafe Buenrostro, a policeman, became the second Chicano detective in Chicano and U.S. mainstream crime fiction. A year later, *The Little Death*, by Michael Nava, was issued and we met Henry Rios, a gay attorney. These two remarkable novels, however, marked the beginning of a new cycle in Chicano/Chicana narrative—crime fiction, but more specifically the police procedural or private detective novel. Hinojosa's second police procedural, *Ask a Policeman*, was published fifteen years later because for him crime fiction is only a thread in the fabric of his literary work centered on the fictional Belken County. On the other hand, Nava published eight Henry Rios novels until he decided to retire Rios a few years ago.

Other Chicano/Chicana authors followed after Hinojosa and Nava. In 1992, Rudolfo Anaya introduced Sonny Baca, a professional PI, in his novel *Alburquerque*. Sonny Baca is the protagonist in four detective novels by Anaya, one for each of the seasons. Also, in 1992, Arte Público Press issued my first detective novel, *Eulogy for a Brown Angel,* and Gloria Damasco, presumably the first Chicana detective in U.S. literature, stormed out onto the crime scene. Until now, I have written four Gloria Damasco novels, the latest, *Death at Solstice,* published in 2009. In 1993, Manuel Ramos published his first crime novel, *The Ballad of Rocky Ruiz,* introducing Luis Montez, who like Nava's Henry Rios is also an attorney. Ramos' Luis Montez series includes five novels.

Hinojosa, Nava, Anaya, Ramos and I form the structure on which contemporary Chicana/Chicano crime fiction rests. It's said that Hinojosa and Nava are the grandfathers, with Anaya and Ramos being considered as the fathers of the Chicano mystery genre. From 1992 until 2005, when Alicia Gaspar de Alba published her remarkable *Desert Blood: The Juárez Murders,* I was the only Chicana writing and publishing detective novels. I suppose that in the genre hierarchy or crime genealogy, I would be considered the grandmother and Alicia would then be the mother, but I've never heard anyone in the male establishment, Chicano or mainstream, talk about us Chicanas in such terms.

A quick look at the Sisters in Crime or the Mystery Writers of America directory is sufficient proof that in the United States nearly half of published crime fiction writers are women. However, the same is not true in the production or publication of Chicana/Chicano crime fiction. Of roughly twenty writers, only six are Chicanas.

From time to time during seventeen years as the only Chicana detective-fiction writer, while at a reading or a signing, other Chicanas and Latinas have confessed their secret desire to write detective fiction someday. Until now, with the exception of *Desert Blood: The Juárez Murders,* and more recently *HIT LIST: The Best of Latino Mystery,* featuring the work of four other Chicana mystery writers, I have seen few tangible results, and I have often asked myself why. What keeps Chicanas (and Latinas as well) from writing and/or publishing crime fiction?

Seeking answers, I began to take a look at my own upbringing, my experiences as a girl growing up in Mexico. I developed a taste for murder and mayhem while secretly reading *la página roja*. When my family and I moved to San Luis Potosí in Central Mexico, I found myself in the midst of a very conservative Catholic community where young and old women who dared to read crime novels were punished or became social outcasts. Some women did read them secretly, making sure their secret was safe if they confided in anyone. Mexico in the fifties and early sixties seems long ago. Although the rules have been relaxed and it is no longer such a *crime* for women to read crime novels, the majority of Mexican women do not read them, let alone write them.

I remember a conversation I had with Sandra Cisneros after my two novels *Eulogy for a Brown Angel* and *Cactus Blood* were published. "I haven't read any of your novels, because I don't like reading that kind of novel," she remarked. I did not give her comment great importance. There are things I will not ask my friends to do for me—like reading or liking my work, attending my presentations or even buying my books. Love takes precedence over crime; however, what Sandra said became relevant when I read an interview in which Rolando Hinojosa talked about having read many crime-fiction authors to learn the craft before he wrote his police procedurals. Like him, I also read many mystery novels as well as author essays on the writing of crime fiction before I wrote *Eulogy*. If anyone is going to break the rules and conventions—and break them I do—we must know first what they are and what the cost, personally and professionally, will be.

Every road taken in my search for the reason Chicanas do not write mysteries kept leading me back to the reading corner. *Sin lectura no hay ni escritura ni literatura*—there is no literature without reading and writing. Suspecting that I was on to something important, I asked Professor Norma Alarcón, who is an avid reader of mysteries by women authors, why she thought Chicanas did not write detective/crime fiction. Without the least bit of hesitation, she answered, "Because they do not read them. *No les han tomado el gusto.* They haven't developed a taste for it."

Since then, I have asked many Chicanas and Latinas the same question. To mention a few, their comments range from "Ugh—*Fuchi!!* No way" to:

"*Ay mujer, es que eso de cargar pistola y andar matando gente* . . . Carry a gun and kill people . . . ?"

"Who wants to write about raping and killing?"

"I'm against portraying women constantly as victims. That's why I don't watch the Lifetime channel."

"We're not like men."

I have walked away from conversations on the subject with some major questions. Do we Chicanas really believe:

1) That since violence has to do mainly with testosterone, it has nothing to do with women?

2) That the constant and at times systematic killing of women all over the world, including Mexico and the Chicano microcosm, is real, but it is not in good taste to write or talk about it?

3) That in truth women are victims of injustice, but it is not okay to seek justice in the public arena?

4) Or in general, that writing crime fiction is neither feminine nor feminist?

Other comments have to do with either the creative process or the value given to the crime fiction genre. I've been told, for example, "It's very difficult to write that kind of novel because it is so rigid." Or "That's not really a literary novel. It's formulaic."

It's true that crime novels in a series may become formulaic. Ideally, each story stands alone, even when it relies for continuity on the same investigator's point of view. But, in each novel, a distinct set of characters, moral dilemmas and ethical decisions confront the investigator. Skillfully crafted, each story in a series will be entertaining yet poignant and emotionally engaging. It will be delivered in a language accessible to a variety of readers, with characters portrayed honestly in all their facets, including those who do wrong. It will deal with moral dilemmas, unethical and criminal acts, but it won't be preachy in its approach to what is right and wrong.

Is the job of the literary writer any different from that of the genre writer? The development of a credible plot and characters and adequate descriptions of the place where the story develops are the basic requisites any literary or genre fiction writer must meet. Writers may choose to fracture time, set the story in the midst of a particular era, counterpoint stories within the larger work, use brevity of detail or indulge in complex description, maintain a tight pace or allow characters moments of reflection. But literary or genre, any writer must answer to the degree necessary five pertinent questions: What? Who? Where? When? Why?

For the crime writer, a sixth question—How?—is paramount, because the investigation of the crime and the quest for justice are the wheels that keep the plot moving and eventually lead, in a full circle, to the motives for the crime and the apprehension or death of its perpetrator.

It's a fallacy that mystery writers make a lot more money than literary authors. So the following comment never fails to make me chuckle: "Maybe, to make money, I'll write a mystery novel someday, but only under a pseudonym."

I do not have the heart to burst these dreamers' bubbles. One crime novel hardly brings in even the five-figure royalty advance in a very competitive field, where you need to establish yourself with at least three mystery novels.

I can, however, assure any Chicana who is now contemplating penning a mystery novel that the writing of crime fiction, when one respects one's art, is as legitimate as any other kind of writing; that exposing the machinations of a "justice system" which more often than not stacks the deck against women, especially women of color, is not only all right; it is also a way to obtaining justice for those who won't or can't speak for themselves.

At times, when I'm writing, I think of my grandmother and her pronouncement that tropical night, long ago that "there is no justice in the world." I regret I never had a chance to tell her that sometimes I write to bring about justice, even if poetic, or that the pounding of her heart against flesh and bone that evening has become the *Andante Vigoroso* of my heart. I want to think that she would be proud of Gloria Damasco, and of me, for giving voice to those who can't speak for themselves.

THE ASPCA'S MOST WANTED: ALL CREATURES GREAT, SMALL AND PEEWEE

MY FAMILY AND I lived in a small town surrounded by tropical forests. The wetlands bordering the Coatzacoalcos River and its tributaries were home to wild and colorful and deadly terrestrial, avian and aquatic fauna. We did our best to cohabit with them and stay out of their way. Shamans and healers were well aware of the behavior displayed by both wild and domestic animals when they were sick or hurt. Based on their observations, *curanderos*—healers—were able to identify and explore the uses of some botanical remedies for a variety of human ailments and conditions that also afflicted animals.

My dad was fond of retelling stories about the healers he had met and the way they had obtained some of their knowledge. At the time, he was the superintendent in charge of the southeastern division of Mexico's National Telecommunications Company, a federal agency. He was also one of its best troubleshooters. When the telegraph lines went down due to natural or man-made disasters, my father and his crew were dispatched to reestablish communications. Sometimes they were joined by teams from the National Telephone and Railroad Agencies. The crews traveled on foot or horseback, in train cars or wagons when possible, or in hand-powered rail

carts when not. They waded through flooded fields and marsh-
es, and crossed Mexico's great southern rivers by dragging
themselves across on rope cables when rafts and ferries were
destroyed by the irrepressibly violent currents. They had to
survive in very unsanitary conditions and were also exposed to
dangerous wild animals and some of the most poisonous
snakes anywhere in the country.

When it was too dangerous to set up camp in the wilder-
ness, they depended on the kindness of villagers in the area for
a place to sleep and some food and clean drinking water. In a
small village in Tabasco, the state southeast of Veracruz, my
dad and his crew were invited to the local *curandero's* home to
clean up, rest and share a meal. This particular healer was a
very good storyteller and soon had them enjoying the tales of
his adventures in the jungle in search of this or that flower,
herb, root or seed, beetle or worm, to prepare his curative
potions and powders.

Once, he had come upon a clearing where two venomous
snakes tangled in deadly combat, their bodies tightly wrapped
as one, fangs ready to strike. Why they fought, he didn't know.
He was well aware that no one could now keep them apart, for
they'd fight until one or both were dead. After a while, one of
the snakes lay lifeless on the ground; the other was weakened
by the struggle and the poison racing through its body. The
curandero followed the dying snake at a safe distance, planning
to remove the small sacs of poison from it after it died. The
snake made its way to a bush that had clusters of tiny yellow
and red flowers, and ridged green pods with small red berries
in them. Some of the pods underneath the bush lay open;
their dried berries were scattered on the ground. The snake
slithered slowly around the bush a few times, then rested its
long body on the bed of dried berries. It lay there hardly moving for hours.

The *curandero* climbed a tree as the glow of twilight was only a thin red line over the horizon. He finally fell asleep. When he woke up the next morning, the snake was gone. He raked the dried berries under another bush with his hands, and picked as many of the fresh opened pods still clinging to the twigs as he could. At home, after drying the small berries, he ground them and made a pink-colored powder. With it he filled a small cloth sack, the size of a pin cushion, and sewed it to a cloth wristband.

The trial of this remedy in places so far from a pharmaceutical lab was done directly on humans who had been bitten. The healer himself admitted that the powder he'd made from those berries had limited use. He had not been able to successfully treat anyone whose blood already carried the most lethal of venoms, such as that of a snake whose bite would make a victim bleed through every pore in a matter of minutes. The powder had the greatest effect on venom that flowed slowly through the bloodstream. He also realized that the powder was most effective when the cushion was tied around the limb affected, at about the length of the injured person's stretched hand—thumb to pinky—above the punctured skin. He gave my dad one of the cloth wristbands which contained the powdered medication pad attached to it and asked that he try it.

My dad never got bitten by a snake but one of his workers did. Others in the crew immediately found the puncture marks, cut the area open and squeezed poisoned blood out. Then they applied the pressure-release method to stop the blood flow for minutes at a time. It made little difference to the man's condition. If nothing else was done, the crewman would be dead by dawn. So my dad tied the cloth band and cushion with the pink powder around his leg in the manner that the *curandero* had prescribed. He became a believer when the worker was still alive—and hungry—by the next day. The crewman told my dad that he'd felt as if his leg was on fire right on the spot the healing pad was placed; he had a fiery red mark there the size of a large coin to prove it.

"This doesn't mean that you can take unnecessary risks," my father emphasized, and went on to teach us how to identify poisonous snakes and what to do in case we found ourselves near one. Among the most poisonous were the *nauyaca* snakes. From two to four meters long, they featured ash- or brown-colored skin covered by rough scales, darker brown diamond designs and a pointed head. In the coral group, the tropical red coral snake reigned venomously supreme with a slim body covered by rough scales and displaying bands of red and black wider than the bright ivory (lighter yellow) stripes.

In all cases, my father's advice was to keep an eye on the branches of trees and to tune into the sounds around us, especially the sound of disturbed dry leaves on the ground. When in doubt, it was best to stand still until we were sure there was no danger. We should always carry a long stick to pat the ground ahead and around us and, with it, poke any object that had been on the ground for awhile, before picking it up. Jumping over an old fallen tree trunk without making sure there was nothing in its hollow, hiding underneath it or on the other side of it was a no-no. Lastly, we were warned never to stick our hands into any hole. But my dad forgot to tell us that snakes could also swim. We learned about it the hard way.

It happened that the town was finally about to get potable water in homes. People looked forward to getting it from the tap rather than having to purchase large cans of spring water from water carriers every day, so they didn't mind having one-meter deep open trenches, where the pipes and drains would be laid. It took only a couple of storms for rain water to collect in the trenches all over town.

On a Saturday afternoon, my dad snoozed in the rocking chair on our front porch while my brother Víctor and his friends used a couple of long, thick tree branches to go down into the long trench in front of our home. Barefooted, they treaded the murky water one after the other in line, pushing each other and laughing. Although I often joined in the boys' games, going down into the murky water, which reached up to my brother's calves, wasn't that appealing. So I just watched the boys play for awhile. When they realized it wasn't as much fun as they'd anticipated, most of them climbed out and headed home. I sat on the edge and watched Víctor still running in the trench. I gasped and jumped to my feet when I saw the pointed head, followed by the wide black, ivory and red bands of the red coral snake swimming about three feet behind my brother. I ran to the porch and woke my dad up.

"Vito is in the trench. A coral snake is in the water, too. Hurry!!"

My dad bolted to the street. He stood still at one end of the trench to look and signaled for me to stay back and be absolutely quiet. Then he knelt closer to the edge. Víctor was heading his way. He'd have to turn at that point to run back to the other end. Víctor waved at my dad and slowed down to make the turn. When he was at arm's length, my dad grabbed him from under his arms and yanked him out of the water. It all happened so fast that the coral snake hardly noticed that my brother was gone before it slowed down.

I was in awe of my father, who took a visibly shaken Víctor and me into the house, poured two tablespoons of sugar into a tall glass of water and had my brother and me share it to prevent susto—shock. A half hour later the red coral snake still swam in the trench. One of the neighbors brought a large sack with long strings he held onto. He lowered it into the water and caught the snake, pulled on the strings and hauled it up to release the coral into the wild later. From that point on, we were all ears when my father talked to us about the different ways to avoid danger.

When it came to home-raised farm animals, for our own mental well-being we were allowed to play with chicks and other baby farm animals out in the yard, but not to adopt them as pets. "Is that chick going to be friend or food?" Abuelita Nico, my grandmother, always asked us.

Bringing any living animal into the house, whether friend or food, was a no-no, and having them sleep with us was totally out of the question. Everyone feared contracting a disease for which there was no cure. Any big or small creature, one-cell and microscopic organisms could quickly become agents of infection for diseases such as malaria, rabies, tetanus or diphtheria. Not counting digestive tract and nervous system denizens, parasites could cause painful infected sores on the skin, scalp, eyes and other parts of our bodies. Great care went into the preparation and preservation of food, especially raw vegetables, pork, seafood and poultry since there was no refrigeration available at the time. Children with highly infectious diseases were quarantined in their respective homes to prevent an epidemic; their personal and bed clothes boiled with plenty of soap. For a week twice a year, the adults and school children in town were given and were urged to take mineral oil or other kinds of herbal laxatives to flush out tapeworms, amoebas and other digestive tract parasites. Health brigades came into town to vaccinate children and adults against smallpox and polio, and to spray stagnant waters with DDT to kill the malaria mosquito.

My mother was bitten by infected mosquitoes and became ill with malaria. She was told there was no cure. Though she was strong and survived it, for the rest of her life she suffered the sudden flare-ups of the disease and its aftereffects, such as her propensity to develop anemia. After a difficult pregnancy, she hemorrhaged and lost the baby, and her blood was depleted of vital nutrients. Since the foods known to enrich blood had proven to be somewhat ineffective, the doctor ordered that my dad take her to the slaughterhouse and carry along a clean mug. The doctor knew one of the butchers and sent word to him he was to sell him a mug filled with first fresh blood from the steer's carotid artery. The choices were either this unpleasant cure or a lifetime plagued by all kinds of liver and blood-related complications. Gagging and shaking my mother drank her mug full of steaming cow's blood once a week, until her color improved and she regained her vitality.

People in town were realistic; we all knew that we only had one another to rely on in case of a disaster or epidemic. Like my mom, no one talked to visitors about the extremes we had to go just to survive, lest we be considered wild and primitive. But we lived in a remote corner of the country. Xalapa, the capital of Veracruz, was a six-to-seven-hour bus or train ride from our town. It'd take anyone about ten hours by bus and twelve on the train to reach Mexico City. Although there was a medical doctor in town, there were no vaccines to prevent or antibiotics to combat multiple childhood and other viral or bacterial infections. So, by age seven, respectively, my brother Víctor, my sister Conchita and I had the measles, rubella, chickenpox, mumps and whooping cough. We had thankfully been spared from exposure to tetanus and diphtheria and had been inoculated against polio and smallpox, but we weren't protected from the knowledge of death. At times we went with our parents to wakes, funerals and to the *camposanto*—cemetery. Every time we were tempted to bring animals into the house, we were told another story of a malady caused by these invisible microbes that were transmitted to humans by sick animals or the pests that plagued them.

In spite of my dad's warnings, my brother Víctor and I broke that not-in-the-house-and-never-stick-your-hand-in-a-hole-in-the-ground rule only once when we brought a baby snake into the house. For days, we observed a nest of a non-poisonous *ratonera*—rat-eating constrictor. When the mom snake was out, we decided to look in the narrow, shallow pit between the protruding roots of a tree and saw a *culebrita*. My brother picked it up, put it in his pants pocket and took it home. Víctor found it a temporary hiding place in a large clay fruit bowl in the kitchen, too deep for the baby snake to get out. As a safe measure, we put back some of the oranges in it and covered it with a colander. We intended to take the *culebrita* out and find it a safer nest in the morning. But we forgot. Machi, the cleaning woman and cook, arrived earlier than expected the next morning. Her screams could be heard all the way to the townsquare the second she reached into the bowl for oranges and felt something cold and slick crawl into the palm of her hand. That same day, my father took us to the place we had found the baby snake and, using a stick we put it back in the hole between the tree roots. We knew that some animal moms abandoned their young when they'd been handled by humans. That night my brother and I prayed to the Virgin Mary that the snake mom would accept her *culebrita* back. To atone for our trespass, we stopped playing with baby animals for a long time.

One day my father came home with Algodón—Cotton—a rabbit, and asked if we wanted him for a pet. He was probably an albino, my dad said, because he was all white and his irises were red. We immediately fell in love with Algodón. It was still early spring and the hottest months were yet to come. So my dad paid one of his crew workers to make a tall chicken-wire cage for our rabbit, under a shady tree next to our vegetable patch and my mom's roses.

We'd never really had pets before, let alone an albino rabbit, thus we thought it was normal that Algodón slept most of the day. Every night, Algodón dug a different escape route and headed straight to the vegetable garden. Every morning, my mom found shreds of lettuce and spinach leaves, half-chewed bits of baby carrots and yams, and rabbit droppings scattered around her roses. But our rabbit would always be back in his cage before my mom checked in the morning. He would look at her with sleepy, innocent red eyes. "Night raids on the veggie patch? Who would do such a thing?" his eyes seemed to say.

My brother and I tried the same innocent-eyes trick on my mom, but it didn't work. Time and again we were warned that Algodón would be given to a family who lived on a small farm outside town if the night raids on the veggie patch didn't stop. Víctor and I brainstormed. What if we made Algodón's cage bigger and planted a veggie garden inside it just for him? My dad smiled when we floated our plan to him. He thought it was a brilliant idea; however, it would only work if our pet wasn't a rabbit. Rabbits were insatiable little creatures, like us children, he said and smiled. The next day, he and a friend brought home a large wooden board that was laid under the cage so our pet would not be able to dig his way out of it. It worked. My mom made sure our rabbit always had just enough to eat. Algodón was getting too fat, she said, and we agreed. All concerned were pleased. At the time, we had no idea that a year later we would be moving to another city, and Algodón would find a home in the famous "farm" my mom had picked for him.

We moved to San Luis Potosí, a colonial city in central Mexico, during one of the coldest Januaries there. The city was supposed to have a moderate climate sure to bring out the beauty of rosy cheeks on girls and women. We had moved, however, from a very warm and very humid place, a few hun-

dred meters above sea level, to a high-plains city thousands of
meters in altitude and with cold and dry winters. Left outside
overnight, steaming liquid gelatin quickly gelled, and the
water in bowls was covered by a thin layer of ice by dawn.

Houses in San Luis were made of brick and mortar or slabs
of rose-colored quarry stone and had tiled floors. Rooms connected internally but also opened onto an interior patio or
courtyard. They lacked fireplaces or wood stoves to provide
relief from the cold day or night. We slept under heavy wool
blankets. My mom and dad had bought thick wool sweaters
and coats for us, but the skin on all areas exposed to the freez-
ing wind became itchy and flaky. Despite the lanolin my mom
would ladle on our hands, legs, face and especially our lips
every night, the exposed skin began to crack, then bleed. The
salt in sweat, the slightest contact with even tepid water or
with the sheets at night brought tears to our eyes, which also
stung as they trickled warm down our bruised cheeks.

That first month tested us in many more ways than expected. We had to learn to navigate unfamiliar streets in a city almost
a hundred times larger than our small tropical hometown. Now
we were called *jarochos*—people from Veracruz—tantamount to
unwelcome foreigners for the *potosinos*—people from San Luis
Potosí. No doubt in any of the *Potosinos*' minds we were different in every way. We did not dress in the day's European or
American fashions; we spoke Spanish with a southern accent
similar to that of Caribbean or Central American coast people; our vocabulary included standard words but also other
terms unheard of in central, colonial Mexico. We lived in the
Barrio de San Miguelito, a neighborhood made famous in a
song for its historical importance, but not because of its resi-
dents' socioeconomic affluence. In my case in particular, I was
not only the shortest and youngest in the fourth grade in a private school, but evidently I did not belong to the same social

class as most of my classmates. We had moved to another city deep in the heart of our own country, and yet, for all intents and purposes, we were experiencing culture shock there.

Víctor, Conchita, Miguel, Guillermo and I didn't complain. We trusted that our parents were right and that the change, despite its harsh and painful beginning for us, was the best for the whole family. In a way, the physical pain and the urgency to find relief for it kept me from acknowledging or trying to make sense of the emptiness in my chest. Every day I looked for tropical green and found the cold blue of the tile and the indifference of the stone around me. We missed our friends. Abuelita Nico was our only living grandparent, but she now lived far away. We had no extended family with whom to share holidays and special occasions. Just mustering up the energy to get ourselves out of bed every morning was a great victory.

Perhaps because we felt so alienated, we became a tight-knit family unit. We found ways to entertain each other, especially under the direction of my sister Conchita, who despite her very young age had a flair for drama and the stage. So we began to work on simple stories. Conchita assigned each of us a role. Sheets and blankets went up as makeshift tents and curtains. A bed became the stage over which we developed our dramatic plots. We used our parents' clothes to dress up. My youngest brother Guillermo played telephone operator, dog, duckling or chick with great gusto. My brother Miguel, with his sweet smile and winning ways, was the good friend, the kind relative, a sage, king or magician. My brother Víctor and I played the adults; I was a parent almost every time.

My mom and dad gave up trying to dissuade us from performing our dramas, as afterwards the beds "looked" made and their clothes were back in their room. They decided it was better to enjoy our shows and our laughter than to watch the mist and dew of nostalgia collect in our eyes every time we had news from our friends or relatives in Jáltipan. A few months later, with the excuse that we needed a guard dog, my father came home with Tonqui, a beagle. I sensed that he wanted somehow to assuage the emotional distress caused by our cultural and physical transplant, and to reward us for applying ourselves in school and being good to one another.

Tonqui immediately adopted my sister Conchita as his favorite companion and playmate. She loved him as much as he loved her, and she began to train him to perform tricks. He was a very smart dog. My sister taught him to walk on his hind legs, shake hands and beg. She wanted him especially to smile, so he could play the role of a human in the next drama. For a month, every chance she got, she gently pulled the muscles of his mouth up to show him how to do it, modeling the gesture and saying, "Smile. Show me your teeth." But he didn't seem to have the least interest in learning how to smile.

"Tonqui will never learn to smile. He can't," my dad told me.

"Why can't Tonqui smile? He's smart," I said in our dog's defense.

"To smile you need the right muscles to make the lips work. Most animals don't have what it takes to smile, or talk for that matter. Tonqui included," he clarified.

I didn't want to disappoint my sister so I didn't tell her the reason Tonqui would never smile for her. Undeterred, Conchita persisted and got my dad's permission to let Tonqui in the room. The day to debut our play came, and Tonqui was dressed in my brother Guillermo's old clothes. On cue, we took our places and began to act our roles under my sister's direction. When it was our dog's turn, my sister prompted him with a whispered, "Tonqui, smile, smile." We all looked at Tonqui. His eyes opened wide. Curving up, the edges of his mouth began to form the long-awaited smile, letting us see his teeth. True, it wasn't the most endearing of smiles, and was actually a pretty weird gesture, but Víctor and I applauded his effort. Not Conchita, who had her eyes fixed on her dog's mouth and trembled as if in great excitement. Tonqui looked at her with wide eyes and again attempted to smile for her. That sent Conchita out of the room and onto the patio.

For days she refused to tell me what was wrong. She stopped playing with Tonqui, who stopped eating and quietly lay in the clean but old coal locker where his bed was. My parents had no idea what was going on.

"Why are you now scared of Tonqui?" I finally asked my sister.

"He has the devil in him, Tonqui does. Did you see his eyes and that scary smile? It was the devil," Conchita said and began to sob.

It wasn't the time to persuade her that Tonqui was just a dog, and dogs were not meant to smile. It was useless to tell her that even if they couldn't smile, dogs were capable of feelings and that Tonqui loved her. So I just comforted her and later told my mom and dad to give Tonqui away because he was just suffering, and my sister wasn't going to change her mind. My dad found a place for him in the country, and we said goodbye to yet another pet we lost to "the farm."

Conchita became so afraid of dogs that she'd break into a sweat whenever she heard a soft or loud, close or distant "grrr" or "arf." My dad had told us many times that dogs, like other animals, could smell fear. And fear triggered in an animal the need to preempt an attack by attacking first. It was best to remain as motionless as possible, just as we had been taught to do around snakes. Conchita tried hard not to show fear whenever we encountered a dog on the way to school, but her phobia won every time, and she used me as a shield. Even in spite of my offering my own leg for the hounds to bite, twice the dogs went around me and sank their teeth into Conchita's. Since the canine culprits were street mongrels, we had no idea if they'd had their rabies shots. Conchita had to have painful anti-rabies shots in her belly every day for two weeks on each occasion.

A few years later, we moved into a brand new home my parents built in a new *colonia*—housing development—almost on the outskirts of San Luis. Conchita had finally learned to control her fear of dogs. She was twelve; I was almost sixteen. By then there were seven of us, and my brothers Jorge and Francisco were the youngest. When my parents talked about getting a guard dog, we all applauded, and soon Yaki, a Belgian shepherd with a great disposition for family living, joined our clan. He became my mom's dog almost immediately and, yet, he also helped my sister get over her fear of dogs completely by walking calmly alongside her when she was on the move and resting at her feet when she played in the carport.

The no-pets-in-the-house rule applied again. So Yaki spent his days on the back patio or on his small mattress in the outdoor laundry shed, attentive to the comings and goings in the kitchen, especially at mealtime. At night, he laid on an old blanket, hidden in the shadows of the carport or the small garden next to it. He was a very wise guard dog and didn't bark at those people he knew were friends or neighbors. But he would growl and charge at the iron fence and gate as soon as passersby or their scents were unfamiliar to him. When he got into a frenzy, my mom soaked a small *bolillo*—a soft French roll—in milk and hand-fed it to him. I never understood how the remedy worked, but I suspected that, like people, Yaki simply needed a little pampering and love.

As soon as I was sixteen, a boyfriend was welcome to accompany me home and visit with me for a short while after

a date. That year, I had my share of dates. I also had many
male friends with whom I was never romantically involved.
Growing up with an older brother, his friends, and with our
older male and female cousins and their friends made it easy
for me to relate to both genders and to older teenagers. My
parents always welcomed my friends at home. They actually
preferred that los *galanes*—young gentlemen—did their courting on a bench in the carport, under their watchful eyes, than
elsewhere. They had a balcony built outside my sister's and my
bedroom so we could enjoy our prospective boyfriends' serenades. It was part of the courting ritual for teenage boys to sing
romantic ballads to the girls whose hearts they hoped to win
or had already won.

Serenades were called *gallos*—roosters—because they happened in the wee hours of the morning when the roosters
begin to announce the rising of a new day, perhaps also
because love always offers the possibility of renewal. In a family that enjoyed music so much, our *gallos* were enjoyed by
everyone, including the birds in their cages next to the carport. But they were not enjoyed by Yaki, who growled, bayed
and barked through the whole singing session. On more than
one occasion, he scared away the serenaders. Those who sang
to us despite Yaki's "accompaniment" were brave and worth
considering, my sister and I agreed.

One night, my brothers could not stand Yaki's counter-
serenade from hell, although the musicians and the suitor kept
on playing and singing. My brother Guillermo took it upon
himself to get a *bolillo* from the bread basket and soak it in
milk. He went outside and showed the group what to do. The
bravest of them, my sister's wannabe boyfriend, shaking down
to his socks and shoes, did the honors and held the wet roll
while Yaki contentedly slurped and chewed. Somehow the
word about Yaki's "bad" behavior had already gotten around

our crowd, but later so had the remedy for it. From that time on, any young man who wanted to serenade "the Corpi girls" was well advised to pay a visit to his local bakery or raid his family's pantry before heading our way.

I was sixteen when I graduated from high school and almost seventeen when I entered dentistry school. I was one of three girls in a class of thirteen students. Although I was a year younger than my classmates, I was always accepted as an equal member of the class. That first year, I marveled at the intricacy and efficacy of the human body, and conversely at its fragility and vulnerability, as we studied anatomy, biochemistry, physiology, did dissections on cadavers and watched autopsies. It was also the year my male classmates taught me how to play chess, ping-pong, poker and canasta. I had my share of requests to go steady with this or that young man. Toward the end of my first year of dentistry school, I met Guillermo Hernández, who was six years older than me. He was an intellectual, fond of philosophy, literature and the belle arts, and he found the social practice of *gallos* bourgeois, ridiculously sentimental and hypocritical. Yet, he also got hold of a couple of musicians and friends and stood under my balcony hoping to win my affection. That year was also Yaki's best as he had breakfast on many a good *bolillo* soaked in milk while the music played at three o'clock in the morning.

Guillermo and I got married three years later and arrived in Berkeley three weeks after our wedding. I was nineteen years old. We rented a studio on Telegraph Avenue. The first time I visited Cal, I was immediately intrigued by some of the young women walking up and down The Avenue, smelling of patchouli, wearing flowers in their hair but no garments under their tie-dyed cotton shirts and long, batik skirts. They walked on bare feet, carried their babies on their backs, nestled in a shawl or a cotton stole tied in the front—like native Mexican women—and breastfed them in public anywhere they happened to be, something that the rest of the Berkeley Hills population found totally inappropriate.

"*Son los jipis*—They're the hippies," Guillermo said. He explained that theirs was an anti-establishment or counter-culture movement. They purposely challenged authority and middle-class materialistic values and etiquette. During that first year in Berkeley I found myself in constant awe of them. First, I was coming from an underdeveloped country where going barefoot meant not having money for shoes. Here not wearing shoes was considered "cool." Second, it was the time when half of the youth in the nation asked for "freedom." Their parents' generation pointed the finger and sneered at "those hippies" and other youth who seemed to "confuse freedom with license" and had no respect for authority, law or social order. Third, we had arrived in California a year after the assassination of John F. Kennedy, and the country was still reeling from that confrontation with violence. In the seconds it took that bullet to hit and traverse President Kennedy's brain, the young United States had come of age. A conflict in Southeast Asia was quickly developing into a full-blown war, and the draft had been reinstituted. In addition to African Americans, other minorities were rising to fight discrimination and the violation of their human and civil rights due to racism.

The hippies' defiance of the status quo included letting the children and the pets run as they pleased all over Telegraph Avenue and the Cal campus, including classrooms. The fountain in Sproul Plaza was later named Ludwig's after a dog that liked taking baths in it. I was amazed that professors seemed unfazed and went on with their lectures while the dogs growled and then finally tore into each other, consequently disrupting classes. Walking through campus, everyone had to be mindful at all times not to step on the dogs' smelly, if organic, waste, while they fanned the flies away with their hands. In my case, at five feet tall, I also had to be aware of larger playful or affectionate dogs that could easily topple me over.

Markets and other grocery stores fascinated me. I often walked into the Consumers' Cooperative market—the Co-op—on Telegraph and Ashby avenues just to look at the variety of cheeses and breads, meats, produce, jars and cans of spices from all over the world and all kinds of trinkets and gadgets. I was particularly impressed with the many shelves of pet food and other items to make a pet's life comfortable. Cats didn't lap up milk or eat leftover fish soup. Dogs did not eat the same homecooked meal as the family. My fascination gave way to distress when I found out that many low-income older people bought and ate dog and cat food because they simply couldn't afford to buy meat, poultry and fish at much higher prices than their pensions allowed.

As much as it would have been nice for me to have a dog, I never pressed Guillermo for one. It was beyond our means. Also, Guillermo and I lived in an apartment house where pets were not allowed. Having observed Tonqui and Yaki at home in San Luis, I was well aware that dogs needed constant human interaction and loving attention. Dogs' "hearts" could as easily be broken as human hearts often were. Without love and care, they grew sad and could even starve themselves to death. Even after we moved to another apartment building where pets were allowed, it was inconceivable for us to have a dog that would have to stay home alone all day, since I was going to school full-time to learn English and Guillermo was working. But I could always count on enjoying my family's pets when we went back to San Luis to visit.

Every time I arrived in San Luis, I found new pets. During one of those summers, there was an injured raccoon—Roqui— my youngest brother Luis Enrique had found at the pool of an abandoned tannery and had brought home to convalesce from an injured paw. A flock of prize-winning homing pigeons and doves raised by my brother Miguel circled above the house on the early winter mornings before Christmas.

When my son Arturo was six years old, he began to spend summers with my family in San Luis. His dad and I had been divorced for some three years, but we wanted him to live, if only for two months every year, with his extended family on both sides, and to learn *el lenguaje*—the tongue—that gave voice to Mexican culture. I had to teach the summer session to be able to afford Arturo's visits with both his dad's family and mine. Each summer, he had to travel by air as an unaccompanied minor to Mexico City, where my mom and my brother Miguel picked him up. But at the end of most summers, I traveled to San Luis and stayed for a couple of weeks, then brought him home to the States with me.

One of those summers, I arrived in San Luis and for the first time in years, there were no dogs. But I found an interesting addition to the pet side of the family. A skinny and long-legged fighting cock had the usual long, pointed spur. No one had bothered to give him a name. I'm not exactly sure why but he reminded me of the famed man from La Mancha, so I named him Quijote. He was friendly enough to the humans at home, but he attacked everyone else, in fighting-cock fashion: talons first.

The next winter, to my surprise my mother, who had always been a dog person, had adopted a cat. Pelusa (Fuzz) was a gray short-haired cat, but quite frankly not a very attractive female. My sister Conchita told me that Pelusa had the peculiar habit of picking up her kittens one by one and taking them up the stairs to my brothers' room. There, in an old guitar missing already half of its face, she would deposit the kittens carefully for the night. By the time Pelusa and I made our acquaintance, most of her litter, once weaned, had been given away. A fluffy white-haired, blue-eyed kitten I named "Algodón," in memory of my rabbit, was the only one left her. According to my brothers, Algodón looked a lot like his feline father. Pelusa was a loving and caring mom to her happy, playful kitten, who every evening would climb up and take possession of the Christmas tree, looking like the Cheshire cat in a twinkling multi-colored "Wonderland." Every time, Pelusa stood watch until my mom got Algodón out of the tree.

When the mother cat needed to go out "to do her duty," my mom made sure the kitten stayed in the kitchen with the door closed. But I began to notice that Pelusa would stand by the open door, especially when the gate to the street was open. After sneaking a look around the carport, she would make a dash for the open gate. Wings flapping, Quijote the rooster would come out of his hiding place and trot after her. But she was too fast for him. At times, however, he would sneak up on her in the middle of the carport. Wings extended, feathers all fluffed up, and head bouncing and turning left-right-up-down, he'd trot and sway, closing the circle on a visibly scared Pelusa. As soon as he heard steps, he would run back to his hiding place, and Pelusa would get back to her kitten. I was utterly intrigued by Quijote's behavior, and the idea crossed my mind that he was actually in love with Pelusa. "Impossible," I told myself.

Early one morning, I was making coffee in the kitchen and heard the front door open, but not close afterward, and then the grating of the front gate. I looked out and saw the front door ajar. Beyond the gate, the lady that helped my mom around the house was sweeping and hosing the sidewalk. As I was helping myself to a cup of coffee, I heard a piercing shriek coming from the carport. I rushed out. Quijote had just dug his spur into Algodón's forehead. A fiery crimson stain spread rapidly across the kitten's head. As the rooster was ready to attack again, Pelusa darted out and lunged at him. He seemed stunned. I grabbed him by a wing and flung him out of the way. He landed on his feet and ran to the garden.

The kitten was running around half crazed, blood oozing from the gash on his forehead, afraid even of his own mom. I had a hard time grabbing and holding him. When I finally did, I took him upstairs to the bathroom, with Pelusa right behind me. By that time my mom was up and she came to see what was happening, my brother Guillermo and I had already cleaned the wound with soap and water. My mom applied an antibiotic cream and bandaged the kitten's head. All this time, Pelusa was on my back, looking over my shoulder at her injured kitten and meowing softly.

I took them both to my bed and let them stay there all day. That night, my son Arturo and I shared the other bed in the room. Pelusa did not move from her kitten's side all night. I woke up at five in the morning and got out of bed to check on both of them. Pelusa sensed my presence and stirred. I reached out to her, hoping that she wouldn't scratch me as she had done before when I'd tried to pet her. This time she purred as soon as she felt my fingers gently rub the spot between her ears for a little while. She looked at me with soulful eyes for an instant, then gently moved away from my touch and closer to her kitten.

I heard Arturo sigh in his sleep and went back to check on him, then pulled the covers over him. I listened in the dark for some time to make sure his breathing was normal and he wasn't about to have an allergic reaction to the cats' hair. As my fingers lightly traced the outline of his head, I became aware of how similar the situation that confronted Pelusa, my mother and me was. My father had died a few years earlier, leaving my mom a widow with four young sons at home to bring up. I was divorced, with a young son at home. Pelusa had only Algodón left. In fact, the three of us were single moms with young offspring at home, alone to fend for ourselves and protect our respective kittens as best we could. My heart got misty and I experienced a rush of tenderness toward my mom I hadn't felt in a long while.

"That Quijote the rooster has got to go. He's in love with Pelusa," I told my brothers at breakfast.

"Ay, *manita*—sis—you're crazy," my brother Miguel said. Everyone laughed.

I too couldn't help a chuckle or two. "Not so. I'm serious. Just look at the way he acts around Pelusa. And he's jealous of her kitten. He wants his 'Dulcinea' all for himself. That's why he went after Algodón."

"Come to think of it, I've also noticed his song and dance around her," my mom said.

"Go to the market and get him a hen. I think he has some species identification issues, this cock," I insisted.

"I don't want any more chickens here. I had enough of them when we had the chicken farm. No. I'll find him a place," she said and sighed.

We all laughed because we already knew what and where that place was. It had always been sad to say goodbye to a pet, even when we had to do it for his own good. We got ready to let Quijote the rooster go so he could work out his identity crisis without causing greater injury to others. The day before Arturo and I left to Mexico City to catch our flight back to San Francisco, an old friend of my dad's came for Quijote, and another family pet ended up at "the farm." I chuckled at the thought that in English "to buy the farm" meant to die. But at least our pets were still alive when they reached "the farm."

Pelusa and her kitten had a run of the house for six months. One day she left and didn't come back. My mom looked for her, but finally gave up. Pelusa had probably been hit by a car and died. We never knew for sure. Algodón seemed traumatized and hardly left the house, until one day when one of my mom's older friends came to visit. She had recently lost her husband. Algodón took to her right away, and she to him. He followed her home. My mom swallowed hard and her voice broke on the phone when I inquired after Algodón's well-being and she gave me the news. "It's all right. They need each other. I still have all of you," she said.

At home in Berkeley, my son Arturo wanted to have a pet, but he suffered from asthma and skin allergies, and any furry friend was out of the question. At that time, we lived in a small cottage with a nice fenced-in yard where Arturo played every afternoon while I made dinner. There were two other cottages in the back, one of them a duplex. Kathy, a Native American grad student at Berkeley, and her boyfriend lived in the lower flat. She had a cat she had named Finnigan (perhaps Finnegan) whom Arturo renamed Figgy.

Figgy and Arturo became pals right away and sometimes played in the yard. Every time Arturo was in the bathtub, the cat scratched the back door and serenaded us with a symphony of meows until I let him in. He never tried to get in the tub, but he would stand on his hind legs and paw the water in the plastic pail Arturo would hold up for him to see. On occasion, he would sit on a corner of the tub and purr. I never allowed Figgy to roam the house at will and escorted him to the back door after my son's bath. The path from the bathroom, through the kitchen and out the back door, was always full of meows and reproachful glances from Figgy, and many an apology from me: "It's not you but your hair. We don't want Arturo to get sick, do we?" I cleaned the area well as soon as my son's feline friend left. It was the only way to preserve their friendship and keep Arturo from having an asthma attack.

When I graduated from Cal, we moved to a small house on 40th Avenue in East Oakland, around the corner from the Hells Angels headquarters. By then, I was also working as a half-time teacher in the Oakland Public Schools Neighborhood Centers. Arturo was in the first grade, but he missed his friend Figgy. One day after school, we stopped at the pet shop. Arturo liked a blue parakeet—Keet—and we went home happy. We finally had a pet for him we didn't have to borrow from a neighbor or to worry about it causing Arturo to lose his precious breath.

Keet was a smart bird, and somehow he always managed to get out of his cage. Every afternoon Arturo and I heard the flapping of wings as we entered the house through the back door. We would find him on the kitchen counter, cooing and preening. He'd always let me pick him up and put him back in his cage. As long as we were in the house, he was content in his home and happily proceeded to clean his beak on the pumice stone. Then, he had his meal of seeds while I cleaned the kitchen counter thoroughly before cooking our meal.

Despite my fear that one day Keet would just fly out the kitchen door and never come back, he was never tempted to explore the outdoors. One day, Arturo and I stopped at the market on the way home. I was carrying my school bag and a couple of bags with groceries pressed against my chest. Arturo had his school bag to carry and couldn't help me. I barely managed to unlock the door without dropping the bags of groceries. As I pushed the door hard with my foot, I heard the flapping of wings, but I didn't see Keet. I left the kitchen door open while I cleaned the counter where Keet had spent the day; I then put away groceries and started dinner.

Arturo came in the kitchen and said, "Mom, Keet isn't in his cage. Where is he?"

We immediately looked in the trees in the yard, in every room, even under the beds and other furniture, but our winged pet wasn't anywhere to be found. I had to call off the search. I told Arturo that his parakeet had probably flown away, but that maybe he would come back. When I finally went to close the kitchen door, to my dismay, I found Keet on his back, legs up, and his small body cold. I had inadvertently killed him when I pushed the door open. After putting him in a small box I found in the laundry room, with trembling hands I hid it outside. The next day, while my son was at school, I buried Keet in the yard. Sometime later I finally told Arturo that Keet was dead and that I had inadvertently killed him. I barely managed an "I'm so sorry."

"It's okay, Mom," Arturo said, trying to comfort me, and asked, "Is there a parakeet heaven?"

"Keet was a good bird, and I'm sure he's now in parakeet heaven."

"That's good," my son said and hugged me.

I marveled at his composure and wisdom even at his young age.

After our home was burglarized, I decided to look for another rental for us. My very good friend and former Cal classmate Arturo Carrillo, with whom I had played chess every Sunday for years, and who was also a real estate agent, helped us find a new place. We moved to a home on East 28th Street near Highland Hospital in Oakland, where my son grew up and I lived for twenty-four years. After the first two years there, Arturo and I finally dared to have another pet.

My twelve-year-old niece Dulcita had come from Jáltipan to live with us for a year so she could learn as much English as possible in that time. After-school music, art and martial arts lessons and other activities for both the kids kept me twice as busy and always trying to catch my breath. Under pressure from both Dulcita and Arturo, I decided to get another pet. This time we welcomed a male hamster into the family. We also bought him a special home, a Habitrail, which helped contain the hair and was easier to clean. Ham spent his nights and days indefatigably running in place in the wheels of his Habitrail. He didn't seem to mind being alone during the day. I'd finally found the perfect pet for us. And yet, I worried that Ham would succumb to loneliness eventually. I wanted him to survive, so I went back to the store and got a female, Lady Ham, to share his Habitrail, perhaps have a family. At first everything went well and we, creatures great, small and pee-wee, were all happy. But I changed my mind when I found Ham's bloody dead body and Lady Ham's face, down to her whiskers and incisors, covered in blood. The evidence was irrefutable: We had a "black widow" Lady Ham on our hands.

Another pet had "bought the farm." I had no idea that the noir story was about to turn into a tale of horror and infanticide as well. Lady Ham had gotten pregnant before killing Ham, then gave birth to six tiny Hammies. With eyes closed they'd grab onto nipples and nurse for a long time, except for Hammy VI, who seemed too weak to push the others and get to his intended and vital food source. He grew weaker each day, and one day Dulcita and I found him with his foot stuck in a corner wire at the bottom of the Habitrail, unable to free himself.

Without giving much thought to the possible consequences, I reached in and had just managed to free Hammy VI when Lady Ham charged at me and sank her teeth into my right middle finger. I cried out in pain. She sniffed the baby, left him there and went back to nursing the others. Not really having a plan as to how I was going to help him survive, I attempted to retrieve him a few times. Each time Lady Ham charged at my hand furiously, and I was unable to do anything.

Without much needed nourishment, Hammy VI died a few days later. Before I went to pick up the kids at school, I risked being bitten and reached in the Habitrail to retrieve the baby hamster's body. Seemingly indifferent this time, Lady Ham looked at my hand and went back to nursing her other pups. I put the body in a paper sack and buried it under the creeping rose in the yard, next to Ham's body.

At least the other babies survived, I told Dulcita and Arturo. But when they were old enough, Lady Ham began to fight with them. I knew she could be vicious and I didn't want to come home and find a massacre. I couldn't afford to buy each of them their own Habitrails, not that we had room for all of them anyway. So Arturo, Dulcita and I decided to give the young hamsters away to the pet shop. One went to Ricky, one of Arturo's classmates and his best friend. The next day, after punching a couple of holes through a cardboard box, I put the rest of them in it, except for Lady Ham. I took them to the pet store and asked the owner, whom I'd gotten to know, to give them to children who couldn't afford to buy a pet. He agreed.

A week later, I took the kids to the pet shop. Most of the hamsters were already gone. While we were there, to compensate for our loss, I told Arturo and Dulcita to choose a couple of gold fish from the aquarium. What could possibly go wrong with fish, I thought. We also bought fish food, the bowl and other accoutrements such as pebbles and fake vegetation to put in it, small nets with handles to fish the fish out, special soft brushes for cleaning the bowl—everything to make our fish happy and comfortable. The kids were excited about their new pets and soon learned how much and when to feed them. The cleaning of the bowl and the Habitrail ("the farm" where Lady Ham still resided in solitary confinement) continued to be my responsibility. I cleaned them thoroughly every Saturday morning while I did the laundry. At the end of the semester, the kids' afterschool activities and additional work commitments and paperwork kept me from cleaning the bowl and refilling it with fresh water for a couple of weeks. The water was getting murkier by the minute, and the fish had their mouths open almost all the time. So, as soon as we got home on a late afternoon, I got to the task at hand, taking the fish out and putting them into a large jar filled with water, emptying the bowl, taking out fake vegetation and pebbles, and washing the bowl and everything else with soapy water. I rinsed everything with very warm water as I usually did and put the accoutrements back in the bowl.

I hadn't kept track of the time and the kids came running into the kitchen in their Aikido outfits, urging me to get going. If they were late to their martial arts class, they would immediately be sent home. I quickly filled the bowl with water and put the gold fish back in it. We rushed out and made it to the dojo with only seconds to spare. Upon our return home, I went to the sink to put the bowl back on the counter, feed the fish and start our dinner. My heart skipped a beat when I saw the two fish floating belly-up on the surface of the bowl. I poked them with a finger to no avail, and then touched the water. It was still very warm, so it had to have been hot when inadvertently I had put the fish in it. They were cooked. I had just made bouillabaisse with our goldfish.

Despite Dulcita's and Arturo's comforting words and attitude, I felt terribly guilty. At least murderous Lady Ham was still alive, even if in solitary, in the small laundry room. When the laundry drain pipe got backed up, the Finleys, our landlord and lady—our guardian angels for they were the kindest and most generous people we knew—came to see what they could do about the drain condition. Mr. Finley asked if he could come in the house the next day while I was at work. He had to get some Drano to open up the drain. Neither he nor I gave a thought to Lady Ham. Hoping to unplug the drain quickly, Mr. Finley had put too much Drano in the pipe and the lye began to fume, then hardened when water was added. The more water my landlord added, the more fumes were produced. He closed the door to the laundry room to keep the fumes from going into the kitchen while he went to get a snake and other tools to break the hardened lye or push it hard to unplug the drain. When I got home, Lady Ham lay dead in the gas chamber the small laundry room had become. "Poetic justice," I said, as I buried Lady Ham next to Ham and Hammy VI, under the creeping rose bush.

A month later I went to the Fruitvale neighborhood Lucky store to get some groceries. On my way in, a young man was holding a can wrapped in glossy paper with the name and address of the local ASPCA and a photo of a sad-looking puppy pasted on it. He pushed the can in my direction. I told him I'd give him something on my way out. He was waiting for me when I walked out of the store. I took all the change I had in my coin purse out and dropped it into the can. He looked in the can then at me, as if expecting me to give him more. I felt so guilty, but I couldn't spare much more since I had only twenty dollars left for any contingencies until the next paycheck. He pushed the can in my direction a couple of times, aggressively, looking disdainfully at me, as if I were the cruelest, coldest person he'd ever met. "A shameless panhandler, he probably is," I mumbled to myself. I quickly pushed my cart toward the parking lot and loaded the groceries into the trunk. Looking over my shoulder, I saw him still staring intently at me. What if he wasn't a panhandler?

"He knows," I thought as I started the car. "He probably has a list of all the pets I've killed. He probably also knows that when I was twelve I used to go with my dad to bullfights

and shout '¡olé!' while the matador fought the wounded bull;
and how at age fifteen, I slaughtered dozens of chickens when
my mom had a poultry farm in San Luis."

I felt a chill run up my spine. *¡Santa Muerte!* I was sure my
name topped the list of the ASPCA's most wanted!

That evening, at bedtime, I read to my son Arturo and to
my niece Dulcita excerpts from the Spanish poet Juan Ramón
Jiménez's *Platero y yo*, the story of the travels and adventures of
a traveling salesman and his donkey Platero as they went from
town to town in Spain, selling their wares. With eyes heavy
with slumber that night, I said a prayer for Keet, the goldfish,
Ham, Lady Ham and Hammy VI, and for all the slaughtered
chickens and slaughtered bulls. Then I fell asleep, lulled by the
memory of my mom's canaries and mockingbirds, the cooing of
my brother's doves, Algodón's munching sounds, Tonqui's
smiles and Yaki's slurps, Pelusa's purring as she groomed her kitten Algodón, the meowing of Figgy the cat as he circled the
tub, and my son Arturo's laughter, and Quijote the rooster's *gallos* as each dawn, he ushered in a brand new day.

COLORLINES: THE KISS
ED OLMOS OWES ME

LIKE THE LEGS OF A RESTLESS ELECTRIC TARANTULA, lightning zigzagged across the dark sky. Bolts hissed and struck the rods on top of Jáltipan's church tower and city hall in close succession. The wind made the church bells toll in wild counterpoint to the thunderclaps right above my grandmother's house. The hurricane was moving inland from the Gulf of Mexico. It would be days before its fury gave way to gentler rain.

I was holding on to my Abuelita Nico's hand tightly. She let go of my hand and headed to her jewelry workshop table in her room, and I followed. My grandmother was a silversmith, a trade that had provided enough to support herself and her two children, my father and my Aunt Pancha. She was also a type of healer, a *sobadora*—a masseuse—and a *huesera*—a bone setter. And sometimes, she would lay the Spanish cards on behalf of a client, too.

My grandmother's skills as a healer and seer, and her wisdom never failed to impress me. But most of all, I enjoyed her stories. Any self-respecting storyteller's repertoire always included a few tales of buried treasure and the spirits who guarded the riches to ensure that only a truly valiant soul or the rightful heir made use of them. But my favorites were her stories about *la muerte y el diablo*, death and evil incarnate.

From different stories, I was able to piece together the profiles of these preternatural beings. They were able to transform into man or woman, depending on the gender of their unsuspecting victims. They took the shape of animals as well, especially black dogs, stallions, cats or birds of prey. Female was *la muerte*'s most sensual incarnation, and male *el diablo*'s most feared embodiment. Darkness was their accomplice. And alleys, swamps and graveyards, dance halls, houses of ill-repute, cantinas, Mardi-Gras balls and gaming parlors were their favorite haunts. But it wasn't unusual to see *la muerte* at the head of someone's deathbed, or hear *el diablo* dressed as a *charro* ride through town on a black stallion, looking to snatch the soul of the dearly departed.

Even at that early age, I was impressed by the large wardrobe the two immortals had at their disposal. Under cover of cloth or darkness, however, the immortals could never truly hide their identity. Silk, cotton or brocade garment removed and the hood or the sombrero pushed back, the skull—*la calavera*—would give *la muerte* away. No elegant shoe nor shiny leather boot or humble huarache could ever hide *el diablo*'s clawed or cloven foot. With merely a look, caress or gesture, Death could kill. But words were the evil one's most powerful tool. With only a few chosen words, promises of abundant riches or success in this life, *el diablo* could convince a man's soul to meet him in Hell and burn for all eternity.

"So he doesn't take the women to Hell, only the men?" I asked Abuelita.

"Not true. He also whispers sweet-nothings in the ears of women, seduces them, takes their souls and consumes their bodies."

"He makes them die? Why?"

"Because he can if a woman listens to him. That's his job."

"Many men dress like *charros*. Are they all *diablos?*"

"Not all."

"So how do you know if a *charro* is *el diablo?*"

"Remember I told you? You have to look at his feet—the cock's claw with a long and pointed spur, and the goat's hoof."

"And what does he say to the women?"

"Ahh. *Bueno*, I don't know. He's never whispered anything in my ear."

"What would you do if he did?"

"I would try not to listen, run home, maybe. What would *you* do?" my grandmother asked, perhaps already aware of what was on my seven-year-old mind.

"I guess I wouldn't let him whisper things in my ear."

"Good girl," she said.

I sighed. I wasn't a good girl. I wasn't a toddler anymore, but "why" was still my favorite word. I questioned everything, and I often eavesdropped on the adults' conversations, a "bad habit" that would land me in a swamp of trouble one day, my mother warned.

I'd begun to develop my eavesdropping skills when I was two years old, at home, hiding under a tall table that resembled a decrepit contraption with a leg shorter than the others. Unskilled in carpentry, my father had made the table stronger, but at the cost of the original workmanship. To hide its glaring imperfection, a long, lacey tablecloth was draped over it. My mother was fond of telling me that by age two I spoke in complete sentences and loved to hide under that fragile table. With an unusually clear voice I greeted anyone who came to the door. On occasions, my mother caught peddlers and visitors peeking behind and under the furniture, trying to locate the source of the greeting, afraid that they were being lured in by a *duende*—a mischievous sprite. It was then that I learned to be still for a longer time than most children my age.

Later, during the two years I spent as an invisible, illegal student at school, sitting in a corner of a classroom, ignored by the adults around, I perfected my camouflaging techniques. Like an iguana, a lizard or some insects, I was able to blend into an environment, undetected by people around me. Being petite, timid and tending to melancholy helped. By age seven, I had learned not to attract attention to myself and to go about my personal business in life cloaked in silence.

Although Abuelita Nico would have probably laughed, I never told her that using my near invisibility I'd scurried around for months, looking at men's feet, hoping to eavesdrop on *el diablo* as he whispered sweet-nothings in women's ears or made promises of riches and power to men. Deep in my soul, I held the secret desire to learn *el diablo*'s language, a desire I would not confess to anyone, not even to the priest at my first confession the following month.

Endless evenings, I sat in a quiet dark room while everyone else slept, waiting, listening to the sounds of tropical nights, hoping to hear the pounding of hoofs on dirt paths or feel the warmth of breath on my earlobe. The night became my territory, a vast empire in my mind, where every murmur, every cry of a human or animal creature, every flickering of a candle flame or firefly, or the batting of wings spoke of secrets and mysteries, horrors and fears. To my great disappointment, that year, not once did I see anyone with a clawing or cloven foot, nor did I ever hear the evil whisperer's seductive speech. Instead, I became a professed disciple of silence.

Throughout my life, no matter where I've lived, silence and melancholy have been my friends and allies. They've aided the internalization of feeling and the introspection necessary to find the variety of incongruent elements in my con-

scious and subconscious mind that eventually come together
to form the poem. Solitude was my best counsel when I had to
consider and decide on parenting strategies as the single mom
of a smart, gifted and charming son, who was also a chronic
asthmatic. Silence provided me with the opportunity to find
in myself the strength to face the many problems that confronted me after my divorce, and to muster up the determina-
tion to forge a new life in a new country, speaking in a language that to this day still leaves the aftertaste of salt and grief
on my tongue. My timidity and self-imposed invisibility, cou-
pled with my inability to make small talk, seemed to turn people off.

Often, I was told by my friends in Berkeley and Oakland
that other people found my quietness unnerving. Not having
the precise words to express their opinions, they simply
thought of me as "weird." Conversely, listening and keeping
secrets were precisely the traits that made me a best friend of
many women and men. "If there were women priests, she'd be
one of the best," my friend Carolina Juárez said, as she introduced me at a poetry reading. When looking at my fashion
choices, my Panamanian friend Berta Thayer was fond of saying that I looked like a "nun in disguise." I was considered to
be a "good" poet, and poets are usually perceived as idiosyn-
cratic people. I seemed to fit in that stereotypical portrait perfectly, so people tolerated my off-centricity, my weirdness, as
long as my poems touched a special chord in them.

Being able to blend into the woodwork offered a vantage
point for the poet and the writer in me, although my habit of
not calling attention to myself kept my work in obscurity for
the most part. I was relegated to the margins of Chicano, Mexican and American literature. I have no regrets for being who
I was and doing what I did then, except for the day I finally
met the actor Edward James Olmos, and he withheld the kiss

to which I felt I was entitled. And my quest for answers to questions also withheld for a lifetime began.

I had followed Olmos's acting career since I first saw him in 1981 in Luis Valdez's *Zoot Suit*. But my admiration wasn't based solely on his solid performance as an actor. Looking at his eyes in photos and TV interviews, I suspected that, like me, he had also learned to make silence and melancholy his allies. His title role in *The Ballad of Gregorio Cortez*, based on the book *With His Pistol in His Hand* by Américo Paredes, con-firmed my perception of the man and solidified my admiration for the actor.

Originally produced by Moctezuma Esparza for PBS in 1982, *Gregorio Cortez* premiered in 1984 as a commercial film in independent theaters in the San Francisco Bay Area. After its commercial release, film parties in private homes and com-munity venues abounded. And Ed Olmos graced most of them with his presence. Oh, my hero! An actor who wasn't full of himself, who was willing to do whatever was necessary to pro-mote his people's history and his own work, who sought justice for those who could not speak for themselves! Wow! My soul and mind were in love! It happened that my *comadre* Haydée, who lived in the island city of Alameda across the channel from Oakland, agreed to host one of the film soirees and invit-ed me to attend.

The possibility of meeting Edward James Olmos thrilled me to no end. All the way to my *comadre*'s home, I exhausted scenarios. But what could I say that the actor and the man hadn't already heard? It all sounded trite and ridiculous, all a fantasy. I knew well that imagined reality is the fertile soil of narrative and the catalyst element in poetry. I was always wary of crossing the line between reality and fantasy as it pertained to my own life. So, I reminded myself that it was better to live the moment, however it turned out.

I arrived early. Most of the guests there were Latinas rang-
ing in age from teens to middle-age, with some seniors among
them. A few men clustered together in the living room. The
dining room table had been pushed against the wall to make
more room for the expected large group. Edward James Olmos
arrived a half hour later. He was greeted by my *comadre* and
invited to sit in the living room. Someone put a glass of
lemonade in his hand. He sipped it while my *comadre* thanked
the audience and briefly introduced him. He didn't eat anything. Then he rose to his feet and spoke briefly about the film
and thanked everyone for helping to make it a success. He was
very serious, his tone almost solemn most of the time. Every so
often he cracked a half smile or laughed softly at a fan's comment, but his gaze remained soulful and distant.

Those of us who wanted our film posters signed by him
queued up. As I stood silently in line, poster in hand, all kinds
of witty insights and compliments stacked up but finally collapsed under their own weight in my mind. Should I tilt my
head and smile? Put my hand on my hip? Small talk was simply out of the question. Whisper sweet-nothings in his ear?
Where was *el diablo* when I needed him?

Finally face to face with Edward James Olmos, tongue-
tied, I handed him my poster. He looked at me briefly, then
turned his attention to the paper. I looked at his gumshoed
feet. I looked at my sandaled feet, too. No hoof or claw stuck
out of his shoes or my sandals. My smile went unnoticed by
him, as he wrote a "God bless you!" With the firm hand of an
illusionist who had performed that trick many times, he signed
my poster and the magic was over.

I walked to the dining room, mortified by my stupidity.
Why hadn't I opened my mouth, said something to him? I
sought the isolation of a place by the dining table. "When all

else fails, eat," I thought and reached for some tortilla chips and salsa.

I eavesdropped on the conversations of the women gathered around the table for awhile. Most of them were young, dark-skinned, with glossy, long, straight hair, clad in pink and blue denim jackets and miniskirts or jeans, or oversized sweat shirts and leggings a la Jennifer Beals in *Flashdance*. Some of the women in their middle to late thirties, approximately my age, wore shoulder-length auburn or ash blonde tinted hair and lots of make-up, and above-the-knee skirts or midi print dresses. The older ladies sported salt-and-pepper or salon-colored silver hair and bright silk pants or skirts paired with jackets with plenty-thick shoulder pads.

I was light-skinned, with a freckled face and arms, hazel almond-shaped eyes and dark circles under them, thin lips and a narrow but long straight nose. I had never colored or permed my naturally wavy dark-brown, long hair and used only mascara. Wearing a midi marine blue linen skirt, a white and navy striped, sleeveless shirt, and matching sandals, I stood five feet tall, slender at the time, and not bad looking, I'd been told.

Ed Olmos began to shake hands with the few men present and kissed the cheek of each of the women in the living room. My heart pranced with joy when I saw him heading in our direction, kissing alike every young and old woman's cheek. Life was merciful! I breathed in deeply and exhaled slowly a few times to steady my heart. I fanned my face with the poster to keep my cheeks from sweating and tasting like briny pickles.

Finally, Edward James Olmos was in front of me. My smile and my blood froze when he took my hand in his and shook it briefly, stood straight and slightly clicked his heels. In a split California second he was moving on and kissing the cheek of every other woman down the line. Stunned, I watched him as he dispensed the last kiss and headed to the front door with my *comadre* in his wake. And he was gone.

I drove home in a daze, with all sorts of questions trashing about in my mind. Surely I had myself brought that on, I thought, letting the voice of the Catholic girl drown the protests of the feminist in me. I had said nothing in either Spanish or English, given him no clues to my identity. Maybe that day I was perhaps weirder than usual, too serious, too quiet or perhaps too intense. Surely I'd worn the wrong kind of clothing, looked like a nun after all. I was responsible for my own misery. Of that I was sure. And *el diablo* was nowhere to be found. The silence I had so comfortably embraced most of my life had been my worst enemy that day.

"Opportunity is a bald head with only one hair on it. Pluck that hair off when you see it or someone else will," Abuelita Nico was fond of saying. Edward James Olmos was the only one who had the answer I needed. But I hadn't asked the pertinent question at the precise instant he withheld his kiss. The opportunity to hear an explanation for his unusual behavior toward me directly from him had trailed behind him and out the front door. The lone hair on the bald head had been plucked off, but not by me.

Teaching, writing and motherhood, all-consuming aspects of my life, hardly allowed me time to wallow in self-pity or regret. In time, the-kiss-withheld episode became a humorous story my friends enjoyed hearing. They offered their own explanations about or justifications for Olmos' odd behavior, and gave me plenty of advice. These capsules of wisdom were prescribed to soothe my injured ego but provided no answer to my real query.

"You know what the old proverb says, *Niño que no llora, no mama*—the baby that doesn't cry, doesn't get fed. Next time, demand your kiss."

"He saw how special and unique you are—a poet . . . . Okay, okay, he didn't know you're a poet, but he probably felt humbled by your presence."

"*Eres chiquita pero te impones.* You have presence."

"He didn't kiss you out of great respect for you."

"Bullshit! Next time, demand your kiss; you deserve it as much as anyone else."

"Better yet, dip him tango-style and French kiss him."

"Maybe it's time to change your style: clothes, hair, shoes. We gotta go shopping."

"Get rid of those navy-white old-fashioned Italian sandals. I don't care if Jesus himself handed you the pair in Rome. Out with them! High heel and open toe for you from now on."

"I know you don't think you're sexy but you are. You just need a bit more cleavage."

"*Y enseña pierna*—Show leg and thigh—Flaunt, flaunt!"

"It's his loss. Who needs him? Forget hi-i-i-m!"

"Best story I've ever heard. Did it really happen or are you just making it up?"

In time also, "The Kiss Ed Olmos Owes Me" became just one more story in my repertoire. I well knew that some stories, like some poems, remain unfinished simply because the writer or poet still lacks some of the experiences necessary to form and inform that particular piece. So I suspected the story of the kiss withheld would always end on ellipsis ad infinitum.

Through the years, I kept up with Edward James Olmos' marriage-divorce tribulations, on-and-off-screen triumphs, and his support and promotion of Latino cinema, literary arts and literacy. As for me, I had stuck to my decision not to remarry and had brought up a son who was an undergraduate at U.C. Berkeley. I had by then published two bilingual books of poetry, several short stories for adults and children in Spanish and four novels in English, whose promotion required traveling to cities familiar and unfamiliar to me.

On one of those promotional tours, I reconnected with my longtime friend Roberta Orona at a conference. Slender, with an olive complexion, long black hair, round face and dark round eyes, a breathy voice and a gregarious personality, Roberta exuded sensuality. Wherever she was, a solicitous suitor made it his business to meet her and wait on her. We had been best friends while we were students and activists at Cal, and later at San Francisco State University where we were both getting our Master's degrees. In the seventies and early eighties, we served on the board of Aztlán Cultural, an arts service organization. We had survived our respective divorces, and our children had grown up side by side for several years. We lost track of each other after she moved to Los Angeles to pursue an MFA degree in screenwriting.

At the conference, we spent two days together, catching up with each other's lives and loves whenever our individual commitments allowed. Our conversation meandered to various affairs of the heart and body, and I reminded her of my Ed Olmos story.

"I have Ed Olmos' home phone number if you want to call him."

"Wow! How did you two meet?"

"We didn't. I mean, I met him like you did, at a *Gregorio Cortez* show in San Francisco. I was in line waiting to go into the theatre and Ed was walking up and down handing flyers to the people in line. I asked him to sign my flyer and he did. I showed it to you."

"Sorry." I dug into my memory, trying to fish out the episode. "I just don't remember," I said. I wondered why I failed to remember something so important but brushed the thought aside. Instead I asked, "How did you end up with his phone number?"

"In L.A., I was working for a firm that had a lot of actors' and celebrities' phone numbers." Roberta paused. "You know . . . maybe I shouldn't tell you . . . "

"That you had an affair with him?" I asked, more curious than upset and expecting to hear all the juicy details.

"No. Nothing like that. Don't be offended, but he wrote on my flyer, 'Your beauty is the pride of our people.'"

I swallowed hard. Unspoken, a question blazed through my mind, its heat so intense, chills went up my spine. I shivered.

Roberta felt uncomfortable. "See, I told you it was going to hurt. I'm just telling you what he wrote. He probably doesn't remember me either by now."

"No, don't worry. I'm way past the hurt."

Driving home, I could think of nothing else but the possibility that Edward James Olmos thought I wasn't Mexican because I wasn't dark-skinned, and that he perhaps had denied his kiss to me for that reason. How could that be? He had divorced his dark-skinned first wife for a light-skinned Italian-American actress? And yet, I felt I couldn't shy away from the skin color issue. I arrived home late that evening, dropped my things in my bedroom and took a long look at myself in the dresser mirror. It was still my face, but somehow the woman staring back at me had changed. I began to wonder how I was perceived by others.

While I was growing up in Mexico and looked at myself in the mirror, it never occurred to me that I wasn't Mexican. No one ever questioned my *Mexicanness* based solely on the color of my skin. Sometimes, telling a bit of family history about my Italian paternal grandfather was necessary when someone asked about my last name, since Corpi was not a Spanish surname. And there I was, the unique sum total of the Corpi,

Aguirre, Constantino, Ramos and of so many other unknown European and Native Mexican ancestral gene pools. In the shadow of the question raised by my conversation with Roberta, it was the color of my skin that mattered, not my intellect, character, not my skills as a poet, fiction writer or teacher, my bilingualism and biculturalism, not my being an immigrant single mother who had made it against all odds, nor any other of my achievements.

Chicana writer Ana Castillo once told me, and I paraphrase, "We become people of color only in the U.S. Only here are we judged by the color of our skin." In my case, however, I was being judged by those with whom I shared a history, literature, culture and language in the United States. Their music was my music. I danced with them to it. Mexican food filled my table for family and friends and comrades in the struggle. I had locked arms with them, peacefully demonstrated for the rights of farm workers to safe working conditions and to unionize, for the rights of any person of color to due process in courts and the access for Chicano youth to an education. I was there when Cinco de Mayo and Día de los Muertos became Chicano holidays, Frida Kahlo became an icon and Culture Clash performed for the first time for a welcoming audience.

I spent weeks going over the significance of what I had just stumbled upon. I had always dismissed with a shrug of a shoulder every instance where the color of my skin or my accent in English had been used to define me as a non-Mexican: The Chinese American cashier at the Co-op market in Berkeley, who upon seeing my husband's surname Hernández after my first name, would tell me every time I cashed a check there that I didn't "look Mexican." The African American youth who bumped into me on a sidewalk and instead of apologizing called me "a White bitch," told me to watch where I was going. He was wide-eyed when I said, "*Oye, muchacho, edú-cate*—Listen, young man, get an education."

The many White people who asked me if I was Irish because I looked Irish and they couldn't place my accent—meaning that I didn't have a Mexican accent in English. Some others asked if I was Argentine. A recently immigrated Chilean exile, who knew I was Mexican because I had just told him so, felt that putting down my dark-skinned compatriots was all right with me. "All these Mexican Indians who come to California are ignorant peasants. They have no culture or education." He was surprised that I felt personally insulted by his biased remarks. After all, I was "different." I could pass for White, and so could he.

By no means was racial or ethnic bias one-sided, however. During the 60s and 70s, to be accepted as bonafide Chicanos, some of the older Mexican-American men, who had happily married "White women" a decade earlier, had a sudden change of heart and mind. They divorced their *güera* wives and sought the company of dark-skinned, younger Chicanitas. In some cases, attempts were made to abduct the children from their previous marriages and take them to live with relatives in Mexico, so they would not grow up as "gringos."

The late Juan Bruce-Novoa, a Chicano critic and professor of literature at U.C. Irvine, posed some questions to me. We were both attending a gathering of Mexican and Chicano poets and writers in Ciudad Juárez. Should I be considered a Chicana poet? How were we to identify who was or wasn't a Chicana/o poet or writer—by Spanish surname? The relevance of the sociopolitical content of their work? Or the language chosen to write in? After all, I wrote my poetry in Spanish, and mine wasn't overtly political or "protest" poetry. He didn't mention the question of color or Mexican looks, perhaps because he was also light-skinned like me. I had no answers to his questions, which then as now were irrelevant to me.

On the other hand, some of the Mexican poets and writers at that same Conference in Ciudad Juárez questioned my reasons for identifying as a Chicana poet and writer. "You're not one of them. You don't look like them, write like them or speak like them."

When I started writing mystery novels, every so often I would hear of some Chicano professor or critic who also questioned my ethnic credentials. My mystery novels have as historical background the Chicano Civil Rights Movement and the indelible cultural and sociopolitical presence of Mexicans in California and the Southwest. Underlining their comments was the unspoken presumption that, by writing about our history and culture, I was usurping a right or privilege conferred only to those Mexicans born and raised in the barrios of southwest USA.

South of the border, it was a different story. Although many middle-class and professional-class Mexicans accepted their *mestizaje*, they yearned to be accepted by Europeans and disregarded their Native Mexican heritage. "Mexico is a modern nation. Why do you Chicanos insist on writing about the Aztecs and Mayas and a peasant revolution? That's the past."

After I told Juvenal, a young poet friend from Mexico City living in Berkeley, that I was researching the life of Malinche, the woman who served Hernán Cortés as interpreter in the conquest of Mexico and the dominant figure in my mystery novel, *Black Widow's Wardrobe,* he remarked, "*Y ahí vas otra vez con Malinche*—there you go again, talking about La Malinche—why is she so important to Chicanas?"

My answer was simple every time: "Knowing all of your history is the first step to self-definition, for nations within nations as for the individuals in them." But this assertion meant nothing to Mexican nationals. Just like my comment at a Congress of Poets from the Latin World in Mexico City fell on deaf ears, as I noted that most of the Mexican women poets in the contingent, including me, had non-Hispanic surnames and were light-skinned. Why hadn't the dark-skinned Mexican women poets also been invited?

These various episodes involving the way Mexicans viewed Chicanos' and Chicanas' interest in and appropriation of Mexico's history and all things Mexican would eventually surface in a conversation between fictional Mexican character Mario Quintero and Chicana detective Dora Saldaña in *Black Widow's Wardrobe*.

"But why is it so important for Chicanos to be accepted by us, by Mexican people?" Mario asked with genuine interest.

"Let me put it to you this way. . . . We Chicanos are like the abandoned children of divorced cultures. We are forever longing to be loved by an absent neglectful parent—Mexico—and also to be truly accepted by the other parent—the United States. We want bicultural harmony. We need it to survive. We struggle to achieve it. That struggle keeps us alive."

I had joined the Chicano Movement, convinced that Mexican Americans were discriminated against almost entirely because of their dark skin, even though we were considered "Caucasians." Mexican culture and language were constantly under siege in the United States. Access to the institutions that would make it possible for Chicanos to succeed equally well as Americans of European descent was constantly denied. Racism brought with it a horde of social ills, with injustice and consequent violence topping the list, and with women and their children paying the price. Some Anglo-American men had no trouble marrying dark-skinned Mexican women. But their attitude toward Mexicans in the U.S. barrios did not change enough to tolerate, let alone, embrace, their spouses' people, their culture or music. They didn't bother to learn their language or fight for equal rights for Mexican Americans in general.

After the conquest, and even after its independence from Spain, Mexico's riches and territory had been coveted by other nations, among them the United States, Great Britain and France. Twice the United States sent armies to occupy the country, and in 1848, after Anglo Texans (temporarily) gave up their dream to remain an independent country, the United States annexed Mexico's northwestern territory and California after the Mexican-American War. In the 1860s, instigated by British and French business interests in collusion with the Mexican Catholic oligarchy, Napoleon III sent the French army to occupy Mexico in an effort to impose Austrian Prince Maximilian as Emperor of Mexico. Their aim was to remove President Benito Juárez from office. A Zapotec Indian from Oaxaca, Juárez was the first and only truly Native Mexican president, elected by popular vote. Napoleon also wanted to gain the northern territory on the border between the United States and Mexico. His aim was to help the efforts of the confederate army against the U.S. federal government. In Mexico, before Napoleon the Third's army was defeated and Maximilian was captured and executed in Querétaro, his soldiers had managed to contribute their culinary taste to Mexican cuisine, their rhythms to Mexican music and their DNA to Mexico's *mestizaje* pool.

In my hometown, Jáltipan, as in other villages and towns in the state of Veracruz, having a non-Hispanic surname was not that uncommon. There had been a third influx of European immigrants to the state of Veracruz. Coffee had been first introduced into the tropical areas in Southern Mexico in the late nineteenth century. But growing and exporting it became a more profitable business in the early twentieth century. Like the Spaniards and French before them, Italian and German men came looking to make their name and fortune in the region, not in solid but in liquid, aromatic dark gold. Large areas of jungle were razed and coffee was planted under the benevolent shade of banana trees. During the first half of the twentieth century, U.S. corporations moved in to exploit the state's rich deposits of petroleum, silica, phosphorus, sulfur and other minerals.

Some of these foreigners either married or formed conjugal unions with Mexican native, *mestizo* and mulatto women. Their offspring and following generations bore their surnames—Glover, Miller, Franyutti, Romay, Perry, Prince, Beauregard and Corpi, among others. The recessive genes from these forefathers showed up from time to time in their progeny's looks.

In my own family, my brothers, my sister and I are all café-con-leche—café-au-lait—to varying degrees, some lighter and others darker. Opposite my mother's claim that we had no "Indian blood" in us, even though my brother Miguel Ángel is dark-skinned with black eyes and hair, was Abuelita Nico's assertion that she was "three-fourths Indian" and proud of it. Her quart of Spanish blood was quite evident in my father's features and skin color, but not so in my dark-skinned, black-haired aunt Pancha.

Abuelita Nico never read the Spanish cards for me. Perhaps she had the gift of prophecy after all and had seen what was in store for me. It was 1964. I was nineteen and had just married Guillermo Hernández-Stevens, who was coming to Berkeley, hoping to be admitted as a student at Cal. As Abuelita gave me her blessing the day before our departure to California, she said: "No matter where you find yourself at any time, among friends or enemies, and no matter the cost, never pretend to be what you are not. Live your life by what you dearly believe in. No pretexts. No regrets." Her words of counsel have guided me through many tribulations, vicissitudes and dark times in my life. They eventually helped me to wade out of the skin-identity bog and onto firmer terrain. The echo of Abuelita's words bounced back from the corners of my memory when I saw Edward James Olmos again, in Los Angeles, more than a decade past the kiss-withheld episode.

He was there as the co-founder and host of the Los Angeles International Latino Film Festival (LALIFF). The film festival had a children's literacy component, at the time geared mostly for elementary school grades. It was 1997 and my first bilingual children's book, *Where Fireflies Dance/Ahí, donde bailan las luciérnagas,* had been published by Children's Book Press in San Francisco the previous year. I was invited to talk to hundreds of bilingual third and fourth graders. I read the story in *Fireflies* to them and signed the copies that the festival had provided to the children. I also talked with them, their teachers and parents individually, whenever possible, during my three-day program.

One of my perks was a free ticket to any or all of the premiering films. I was in line in the courtyard of the old Chinese Theatre with many other moviegoers, waiting to be let into the projection hall. At a distance, I glimpsed Edward James Olmos walking to the front doors. I followed his every step. I then looked at my feet as I had once done many years ago. Still no claw or hoof, I thought and smiled. I heard the voice of a woman calling my name and looked for her. My friend Roberta Orona was there, waving at me. I was delighted to see her. I couldn't help wondering what Karmic connection existed among the three of us that brought us together in some way or another, time and again. Roberta and I talked briefly before she decided to get a ticket and hang out with me instead of going home. We went into the theatre. To my surprise Olmos was introducing that particular film and talking about the cinematography used by the director of the film, who was also present. Roberta smiled when I reminded her of the kiss-withheld episode.

After the show, Roberta went to talk to the guest film director. I saw Ed Olmos standing by himself in the courtyard. I did not feel exhilarated or nervous. With clawless, hoofless feet I approached him. Calmly, I smiled, extended my hand to shake his and in Spanish I said: "It's a pleasure meeting you, Mr. Olmos. I am a great admirer of your work." He uttered a "gracias." Without further ado, I turned around and joined Roberta.

"After all these years, imagine, all I did was express my admiration for his work. Yep. No use reminding him of a memory he has no memory of," I told Roberta. We both laughed.

The next day, I had lunch with Paulina Quintanilla, the coordinator of LALIFF's youth literacy program, and with her gracious mother. I asked Paulina if she would forward copies of my novels to Edward James Olmos if I sent them to her. She agreed. Upon my return to Oakland I did as promised. I never inquired from Paulina if she'd been able to deliver the books to him. Being a very reliable and professional person, no doubt she had.

In the end, it mattered little if he ever got them, read them or remembered the episode of the kiss withheld. My books were meant as a gift for what Ed Olmos inadvertently did for me, worth more than a mere kiss. His behavior toward me forced me to accept my reality as a poet and writer and to reaffirm my right to write about anything I chose, regardless of the color of my skin. I regained my sense of self as a bilingual bicultural Mexicana and a Chicana, embracing again in the process who and all of what I am—no pretexts, no explanations and no regrets.

The book on Ed Olmos and the kiss withheld was finally closed.

Future author and past book burner, Lucha Corpi, 1945.

Jaltipán de Morelos, Veracruz.

El cerro de La Malinche.

Dad and Abuelita Nico, Nanchital, Veracruz, circa 1935.

A first family portrait.

Waiting for Tirso "el aguador," Casa de los Aguirre, Jáltipan.

Forever pals: Lucha and Víctor at Abuelita Nico's home, 1947.

With Mom at the Casa Amarilla, Jáltipan, 1953.

At Abuelita Nico's house, 1956.

A new school, a new beginning. Lucha and Víctor, San Luis Potosí, 1954.

Lucha with mom and dad at her high school graduation, San Luis Potosí, November 1961.

Yaki's domain and the Corpi girls' balcony, San Luis Potosí, 1962.

A last family portrait with Abuelita Nico, 1963.

The "Corpi Girls" Conchita and Lucha, 1964.

(R-L) The Rodríguez-Nieto, the Kalmans and Chuck
Afflerbach, Berkeley, 1990.

My wedding reception with Mom and Carlos Gonzales,
Oakland, 1994.

Clinton Park School ESL faculty team, (R-L) Joli, Vivian, Jean, Gail and Lucha, Oakland, 2004.

Aztlán Cultural/Centro Chicano de Escritores Retreat, Mendocina, California. (Center) Francisco X. Alarcón, (L-R) Carolina Juárez, Martaivón Galindo, Barbara Brinson Curiel, Rodrigo Reyes, Bernardo García, Lucha and J. P. Gutiérrez.

Craig Howard, Quincy Howard and Frieda Molina, Chicago 2009.

Corpi Constantino siblings: (L-R) Miguel Ángel, Guillermo Alonso, Jorge Alberto, Francisco Javier, Luis Enrique, sitting (L-R) Conchita, Lucha, Víctor, San Luis Potosí, July 10, 2010.

Standing (L-R) my son Arturo, my grandchildren Kiara and Níkolas, sitting, my daughter-in-law Naomi and my grand-daughter Kamille, Houston, 2012.

MORPHEUS UNBOUND: BUTTERFLIES, MADMEN AND DEATH DREAMS

OUR ROOM IS DARK. *My parents speak softly in their bedroom. My sister Conchita sighs in her sleep in sync with the sound of the breeze streaming in through the window shutters. The mosquito nets over our beds flutter lightly, and their gentle sways tug at an indistinct memory in me. It's more like a recollection of a feeling of something frightening but comforting that happened years ago, when I could feel but not speak. My parents' voices in the next room make me feel that everything is all right, that I am safe in this new home they have built for our family.*

Long before we moved into our new home, we had already begun to call it "La casa amarilla" because my dad had insisted on painting it a bright yellow, a color sure to withstand the hot tropical sun. It stood in the middle of a corner lot. While it was being built, we lived in a house rented from our aunt Violeta Aguirre. For that reason, we called the rental "La casa de los Aguirre." Víctor, Conchita and I had been born there.

We lived in a telluric region that extended from the Gulf of Mexico coast to the Pacific coast, and north to Mexico City and south to Guatemala. Our *casa amarilla* had deep, strong foundations, enough to withstand the brute force of an 8.0 magnitude earthquake, my parents proudly told us after we

123

had moved in. At home, we rested on the confidence that we could survive the inevitable disaster.

Next to our home and directly across from the Aguirre house there lived Doña Macedonia de la Rosa—Doña Mace. Her house was situated at the back of the lot. In its front, overgrown yard, tropical almond trees provided shade to a number of weedy milkweed plants, a favorite of butterflies. She had two grown sons. The youngest was Andrés, *el loco*, the madman who lived next to the house in a padlocked room with only one window facing the street. His mom saw to his daily toilet, hygiene and shave. At times, Doña Mace would forget to lock the door to his room, and Andrés would wander the streets. My dad talked his concerns over with Doña Mace, who reassured him that Andrés would never harm anyone, especially us, the children. My father erred on the side of caution and had a six-foot brick fence built on that side of our property to keep the madman out of our backyard.

On occasion, when we played outdoors, I'd seen Andrés peering out his small window with both hands wrapped around the bars on it. He never wore a shirt, not even when the cooler northern wind swept through town. *El loco* Andrés was at his window the day the butterflies emerged from their cocoons and took their first flight.

"The metamorphosis from caterpillar, pupa, to beautiful winged insect is one of the greatest wonders of nature," my third-grade teacher had said and asked that we watch for this "prodigious" event in nature when we had a chance. And who in Jáltipan wouldn't get a chance? We lived in the midst of tropical exuberance. Some caterpillars fed from the leaves of large bushes. They grew up to four inches long, depending on the body size and wingspan of the butterflies they would one day become. Making whip-cracking noises or having toxic colorful hair or spikes helped them to fend off hungry predators or deter curious children. Thankfully, most of the caterpillars in Doña Mace's lot were skinnier, smaller, with brown or tan bodies and orange or black-and-blue stripes, and they fed from smaller leaves.

My brother Víctor and I paid frequent visits to Doña Mace's yard. We were thrilled when we saw that the butterfly moms had already laid their tiny eggs on the shady side of tropical milkweed leaves. Soon, there were dozens of caterpillars, insatiably munching on leaves from the very instant they hatched. They grew larger and larger until they could hardly move. Then, they began to make dark brown and blue or black cocoons. They spun their threads around themselves and finished just about the time they fell asleep inside their silky yet strong time capsules. They slept despite the heat and humidity during the day. They slept oblivious to the stars twinkling far above them at night, the fading of the moon and the morning star at dawn, and to our daily vigil.

Finally, on a day in late-Spring, the caterpillars were taking flight as neonate butterflies. Víctor and I were beside ourselves the moment we saw a butterfly hover in front of us. We had anxiously waited for that moment. We were home for lunch and had to get back to school for the afternoon session. We took off our socks and shoes and left them with our schools bags inside the front door, then hurried to the lot. *El loco* Andrés was of course watching us, as I knew he would. But we were determined to let nothing keep us from witnessing the first flight of the "winged insects of great beauty though ephemeral life." Dozens of brand new butterflies fluttered over the milkweed bushes or were sucking nectar from tiny red, orange or yellow blossoms. Easing onto the ground we slowly stretched our arms out and let the young flyers set down on our open palms and tickle our ears and faces, until we heard my mom calling us to lunch.

My mom insisted on proper table etiquette, so we washed our hands, faces and feet well. We put our socks and shoes back on before we joined her, my sister Conchita and baby brother Miguelito for lunch. My dad was out of town, and he would not be home until late afternoon. My mom pointed to our plates of food already on the table. Miguelito was sitting in his high chair and Conchita at the table, waiting for my mom to finish cutting her piece of chicken into small bites. I took my seat next to her, facing the doorway to the kitchen.

I was raising my first forkful of rice up to my mouth when I caught sight of a large shadow, like the reflection of a huge crucifix cast on the kitchen wall. Was Jesus coming to visit us, carrying his cross on his back? It couldn't be Him, because Lent had already passed. Was it *el diablo* who had finally decided to pay us a mid-day visit? I shook my head as I watched the T-shaped shadow with a round ball on top move down the wall toward the doorway. My hand was shaking, and I spilled rice on the table. My breath got caught in my throat when I saw the shadow materialize into a man. Standing in the doorway between the kitchen and the dining room, bald headed, clean-shaven, shirtless, barefooted, his unbelted pants hanging just below his hip line, his hands wrapped around a thick stick behind his neck, the madman watched us with unblinking eyes.

As I got up, I pushed my chair back, and it crashed onto the floor. My brother Miguelito fussed. I looked at him. "Pick up your chair," my mom said, not looking at me. My knees felt weak, but I managed to get next to her and pulled on her sleeve several times. When I finally got her attention, I was panting so hard I could no longer talk so I just pointed in the direction of the madman.

My mom got Conchita down from her chair, grabbed her hand, put it in mine and squeezed so I'd hold onto it. "Get out!

Now!" she told us and Víctor, while she pulled Miguelito out of his chair and began her sprint with him to the front door. My brother Víctor, however, seemed to be frozen in place, his eyes fixed on the madman. "Run," I said to him. Before reaching the front door I looked over my shoulder to make sure my brother followed. I saw him lying on his belly with the madman just a few steps from him.

"Get up!" I shouted, but I couldn't help him. I had to take my sister to safety.

"*El loco* has Vito," I told my mom.

Pointing at my younger siblings, she said, "Take care of them." Her voice betrayed no fear, but her hand shook as she took both of her shoes off, held each one by the tips with the heels up, then ran up and disappeared into the house.

I was left to look after my two siblings. I held them tightly against my body, until I heard Conchita say, "You're hurting me," and I eased my grip on them.

My mom finally called us all back in. We found her in the kitchen, washing, pat-drying and applying some ointment to Víctor's elbow. Tears were running down my brother's cheeks. Conchita went up to my mom and put her arms around her while I helped Miguelito up and latched the high chair's tray in place. I went to Víctor and rested my forehead on his temple.

"Did *el loco* hit you? Did he?" I asked in a whisper.

"No. He picked me up. I thought he was going to hit me, but he just left."

Shaken and confused, two hours later Víctor and I were on our way back to school. Having a dreadful confrontation with a madman was no excuse to miss school, in my mom's opinion. I sensed she also wanted us out of the house in case *el loco* came back. The thought of her and my siblings being alone in the house filled me with anxiety until my dad showed up at school to walk us home. Later, while we all sat on the porch after supper, I asked my parents what made a man go crazy and whether Andrés had been born that way.

They shook their heads. "He helped Vito up. Maybe he's just a little crazy, not much," I said.

"He's not altogether there," my dad warned, tapping his temple with his index finger. "He can't be trusted, so stay away from him."

"A woman gave him moonflower tea to drink and put a spell on him. Then, the woman's husband put some finely ground glass in Andrés' drink and he almost died. And people say that he almost killed the man, and that's when he went mad," Víctor blurted out.

"Who told you that?" both my parents asked in unison.

"That's what Doña Mace told another lady. Is that true?"

My parents looked at each other.

With a tilt of his head my dad deferred to my mom, who explained, "Maybe what Doña Mace said happened is true. We really don't know. But that's what she and other people in town believe. Regardless, it's best if you don't go near him or his house."

My parents used everything at their disposal to keep us safe. The windows already had wrought iron bars on them; the kitchen and front doors remained locked at all times. Twice after that first episode, Andrés the madman wandered into our yard during lunch and stood outside our dining room window, trying to dislodge the bars on it. Each time, he went back the way he'd come. One time, we heard Doña Mace's harsh words, the slam of a door, the sounds of a hand against flesh first, then the click of the padlock. *El loco* didn't try again to sneak into our yard, and we never went back to the lot to watch the butterflies.

That first of the madman's visits had lasted maybe just a few minutes. But for me it had been a terrifying eternity. The day of the butterflies, a day of wonder at a prodigious event, had turned into a horrible, unforgettable experience. It marked the beginning of the nightmares that populated my sleep for months, and like bouts of a recurring blood fever, made me wake up in a cold sweat throughout my life: In my dreams, someone pursued me, and I'd run fast then faster to get away from that malevolent, faceless presence. I'd wake up panting, sweating and praying. Sometimes, my arms became wider and thinner and feathers grew out of them. I'd run faster and faster to the edge of a cliff, then jump to take flight. The thrill in my stomach would turn into fear when I felt as if someone was plucking my feathers one by one. Only my own skinny, weak arms were left to keep me airborne. I then plummeted toward a whirling dark hole, waking up with a start just before I was swallowed by that ominous darkness.

Months earlier, after listening to my grandmother's tales of buried treasure, ghosts and the devil, I had lain awake in the dark, waiting for *el diablo* to show up so I could see him and hear what he had to say. But he never made his presence known to me. In time, I was convinced that the devil didn't exist or I was of little importance for him to bother with me. Regardless, I never had any nightmares involving the devil, perhaps because I realized that the evil whisperer really existed only in the world of my grandmother's stories. But not the creatures that pursued me in my nightmares. I sensed more than knew that they could do me more harm than any bad person or devil ever could, because they lived inside my head. Trying to forget them was useless. It made me remember and fear them even more. I didn't want to learn my nightmares by heart, like the poems I'd memorized in the third grade or the details of a crime I'd furtively read in the newspaper, which never caused me to have a bad dream.

Bad things didn't seem to happen to anyone in the family on purpose. My father felt that good and bad, happiness and suffering balanced one another, so we atoned for a bad deed, for instance. Maybe bad situations, like blessings, just happened to people at random. Routine was supposed to be a good thing, my father used to tell us. It made daily life easy to manage so we could concentrate on other important or exciting things. When my brother complained about being bored, my dad told him, "Then go and find a good, constructive way to entertain yourself." Yet, the following Saturday my dad came home with sheets of red tissue paper, strips of light fabric and thin, long wooden sticks we could use to make our own kites. After a great effort, I finally succeeded at getting mine to fly for awhile, and I was happy. But the feeling didn't compare with the frustration for having failed so many times.

My young mind began to wrap around the notion that failure seemed to be more important than success, unhappiness than happiness, insult than compliment, and bad dreams than good dreams. I'd noticed that everybody talked about the injuries to the ego or the body someone had inflicted upon them, rather than talking about the good things someone had done for them. Being aware of my dislikes and likes wasn't going to help me hatch a plan to escape from scary dreamland. Learning to unlearn my dreams seemed to be the way out, but how? I trusted my grandmother could come up with a good plan or an herbal remedy, maybe one of her teas, which could help me out. So I went looking for her and asked her if she had any *yerbas* that could help me.

As usual, she lowered her head and gave me what seemed to be a casual but amusing glance over her reading glasses. "It depends on what you're trying to forget," my grandmother finally said.

"Bad dreams," I replied in a whisper.

"I see." Abuelita Nico thought for a while then said, "Before you go to sleep every night, repeat a few times, 'My dreams are not real. I'm not scared of them.'"

Her mantra worked for awhile, but the creatures pursuing me kept showing up from time to time. I still woke up gasping for breath or pushing away an invisible attacker. Frustrated, I decided that my only recourse was to do nothing, let the creatures run amuck every night and finally get tired. Soon I began to notice that I wasn't as afraid of the entities in my dreams as before, and that pleased me. Maybe now I had a chance to make them my friends. But one night they just stopped their nightly visits. It would take a couple of years for my nightly pursuers to come back, but when they did they were frantic.

Their reappearance coincided with our family relocation from Jáltipan to San Luis Potosí, where my siblings and I had to face many unknowns and possible dangers. I now lived one-thousand-eight-hundred kilometers away from *el loco* Andrés. Not that he could possibly harm me anymore. He had died in an institution for the insane a year after the day of the butterflies. Doña Mace had him committed when she realized she could no longer care for or control him. "*Se lo llevó la tristeza—* Sadness took him," my grandmother said. But the creatures that Andrés' intrusion in my life had created still lived in me, and all I could do was to put up with their unwelcome but expected nightly visits.

During the day, with so much happening in my life, it was easy to forget that they were hiding somewhere in me, waiting for me to close my eyes. After seven years of trying to fend them off, I decided to make a pact with them. Before going to bed, I would simply say, "You can come and go as you please, but you can't rob me of my sleep." My mantra worked, although every so often, close to waking time, I would still be startled awake.

Once, while reading in the school library about some of my favorite Greek myths, I came across the story of Morpheus, the shaper of dreams, and his nocturnal progeny: hallucination, night, darkness, hypnotic trances, death as male and female, fates, insanity, gloom. This Morpheus was serious business, a powerful god in the underworld, who commanded one of the scariest mind-controlling armies. It was obvious that I had my own Morpheus-type in my head. Until then, it had never occurred to me that I could have any power over my dreams. What would happen if I pretended to be Morpheus? Would I be able to shape good dreams for myself? Every so often I succeeded and had pleasant dreams. I didn't remember them as clearly as the most distressing nightmares, but they somehow made me feel undivided—complete.

My free-fall dreams morphed into other kinds of anxiety dreams, recurring much like themes with variations during my adolescence. I was glad a classmate had told me about her anxiety dreams, which were similar to mine. Some had to do with my being late to a very important appointment or a final exam at school. I hadn't studied for it. I wasn't able to even find the room or building where I was supposed to be. Then followed the "not your home" dreams, which seemed to develop along similar lines. I'd go about fixing up and cleaning an abandoned dwelling, which didn't look at all like my real home. In my dream I was always certain that it was my home, until someone came to the door or alerted me to the fact that the real owner was on her way there. I'd walk onto a street in a strange neighborhood, unsure which path led to my dream home. Passersby went about their business without even a glance in my direction.

In some disturbing dreams, I used to find myself either scantily dressed or totally naked outdoors at a place usually unfamiliar to me. Although I couldn't see the people, I felt their eyes fixed on my bare body. My breasts covered with one arm and hand, my other hand over my crotch, I swept the area, trying desperately to find something to hide my nakedness. Sometimes there was an old rag or dingy-looking towel on the ground. The mere idea of having to use a dirty cloth to cover my body was disgusting. But it always got worse when the creatures in my underworld punished me by not providing even a dirty cloth to hide my nudity from the voyeurs. So, on one occasion, I just gave up. Letting my arms down, I stood alone and vulnerable, feeling the cold heat of strangers' eyes on my body. As if touched by a magic wand, my fear and anxiety seemed to lift, then dissolve in the air of my dream. The feelings I experienced the moment I lowered my arms and let myself become vulnerable were liberating. In the morning, I sensed more than knew that I had just found the courage to face the worst of my anxiety dreams.

In the more amusing Morpheus-produced series, I had some funny, intriguing escapades, necking with young men I wasn't particularly attracted to in real life in the back of a car, on a deck or by a pool, but always under the cover of darkness. The feelings were delicious, and I enjoyed them, but I didn't talk about these dreams with any of my classmates. At the time, I never talked about any of my dreams with anyone.

As time went by, I began to understand and accept that my fear defined me as much as my courage to confront its challenges. These dreams were not triggered by any negative experiences or dangers in my present. Somehow my subconscious seemed to interpret certain events or experiences as tests or challenges that inevitably triggered the nightmares. Perhaps Morpheus and his progeny were trying to teach me the lessons needed to survive in life. I also suspected that their recurrence had something to do with a fear of the unknown, an abstraction that manifested itself as a hodgepodge of ineffable notions, intangible images and other sensations perceivable only through the senses in a subconscious way.

I was sixteen and smart. I definitely had a will of my own matched in every way by both my intellect and intuition. All of them, were trying to guide me to a place in my consciousness where I would finally learn who I was, what to do in life. Perhaps there was something beneficial in the dream process, some lessons to be learned from it. I had come close to figuring out something about myself. But I could not begin to put those feelings and notions into comprehensible language. I couldn't yet figure out how to make good use of them.

About a year after the naked-in-public dream, I became aware that the nightmares and anxiety dreams had ceased. It was the year I met Guillermo Hernández, whom I'd marry three years later, at age nineteen. Although I wasn't physically attracted to him for about six months after our first meeting, I enjoyed talking with him, and the devil's love worm wiggled through my ears and into my mind, then my heart. Perhaps people were right when they said that love conquered everything, including unruly, willful, dream-world creatures. But their reappearance after a four-year hiatus, during which I hardly had any dreams worth remembering, was even more terrifying than at any time earlier.

This new development coincided with my relocation to Berkeley. Being a newly arrived immigrant in California, I was far away from my family and all that was familiar and comforting to me, including the language. It meant coming face to face with the greatest unknown of my life thus far. The recurring nightmares triggered by that first encounter with *el loco* Andrés in my hometown returned. Again, I often found myself diving into a dark bottomless pit, and on occasion I could get a glimpse of a very thin glowing rope holding me up and keeping me from sinking into the darkness. I found this

new development as intriguing as it was amusing. Had I finally won Morpheus's compassion? Was he providing me with an
emotional bungee cord as a reward for my courage?

Confiding in anyone had always been something I didn't
think wise to do in San Luis, let alone in Berkeley. On occasion, Guillermo had mentioned to me that I often mumbled in
my dreams but he couldn't make out what I said. Just a bad
dream and already forgotten, I'd reply every time. He accepted my explanation as if my sleep-talking was no big deal, and
he even found one in particular quite amusing. About a year
after our arrival in Berkeley, asleep, in an anxious tone yet
clearly enunciated, I kept asking, "What time is it? I'm going
to be late." In the morning, Guillermo told me about it. It was
the first time that I had spoken English in my dream. To him,
it clearly signified that I was now thinking in English, a first
step to learning it well. We were both happy about it. For me,
it also meant that I would have to negotiate with the creatures
in my dreams in two languages now.

In late 1965, we were subletting an apartment on Ashby
Avenue in Berkeley. One night, Guillermo was awakened
when I sat up in bed, eyes still closed, and with a softly voiced
urgency said in a well-threaded sequence in English: "You
want to kill me. I know it. But you won't. I won't let you do
it." I fell back, still asleep, on my pillow. As if from far away I
heard Guillermo trying to reassure me that he wasn't trying to
hurt me, then asking, "How can you even think that?" I had
woven his comment and question into the fringes of my
dream, and both had gone unacknowledged.

Guillermo's inquisitive glances the next morning showed
his unvoiced concern for me. Seeing no other choice, I confided in him and explained that in my recurring dreams, I had
always run from my unknown assailant. This time, however, I
had decided to stop, turn around and face my pursuer. I reas-

sured Guillermo that my nightmares had started long before I met him, and had nothing to do with him. We never again talked about them.

Months earlier, we had discussed the subject of having a child, but somehow the time hadn't seemed auspicious. By 1966, our relationship and financial situation were both stable enough, and we decided it was a good time to start a family. Six months later I got pregnant. With the exception of two weeks of morning sickness, my pregnancy signaled the beginning of one of the physically and emotionally healthiest and happiest periods of my life. I feared that Guillermo would be unable to participate in my pregnancy, and I wanted to make him a part of it. So, frequently I lulled him to sleep by reading to him from a book on pregnancy and the development of the fetus, our baby, at every stage of gestation. I didn't want to give him any chance not to love his son or daughter or to become part of his or her life. Proof that everything in my life was working in harmony was the absence of nightmares during those months and the subsequent two years. I sensed that Morpheus's progeny were not gone for good, and in a nonsensical, odd way, I missed them every so often. Nonetheless, I enjoyed having the opportunity to start my lifelong journey as a mother in a more peaceful interior environment.

In 1968, when Guillermo became a student at Cal, I got a job as a full-time stenographer in the Wells Fargo Bank's Trust Department in San Francisco. Arturo wasn't yet a year old. My life became a series of predictable daily schedules and routines: Up at 4:30 in the morning; feed Arturo and get him and things ready for his babysitter, shower and get dressed for work, pack everyone's lunch and have a bite to eat before running out the door to catch the San Francisco AC Transit bus at 6:30 a.m. Work from 8 to 5. Get back home at 6:30 p.m. to prepare Arturo's meal and feed him, take out the frozen main course for the day I cooked on Saturdays, sit down to dinner with Guillermo, play with Arturo, give him his bath and sing him to sleep, get things ready for the next day, and go to bed, prepared to do it all over again the next day, for $365.00 a month. My Saturdays were laundry, shopping, cooking and housekeeping days. Sunday mornings were for quality time with Arturo, and with both he and Guillermo during our family outings those afternoons. It required more creativity on our part, but we found ways to keep our love life alive to mutual satisfaction.

During 1968, the creatures in my dreams hibernated. Perhaps they suffered as much from exhaustion as I did. At least the five hours a night I slept were solid. Perhaps they were lulled by the hum of the bus engine or the stories echoing in my mind from the books I read to and from work. The commute traffic gridlock on the Bay Bridge gave me a chance to catch a snooze. But I frequently gave it up in favor of reading, since I hadn't much time to do that at home. That year, I read all of George Bernard Shaw's plays. A *Talk with Mothers* by Bruno Bettelheim turned out to be the most helpful of the child-rearing books I read. I also enjoyed all of Pablo Neruda's poetry and popular novels, among them *Valley of the Dolls* and *The Arrangement*, which I'd seen other women reading on the bus.

When the opportunity arose, I got a job as a bilingual secretary at The Center for Higher Education at U.C. Berkeley. I was thrilled. It meant not having to commute, having more time for my son, one more daily hour of sleep for me, plus a large increase in salary. Guillermo worked part-time for Stiles Hall, off campus, and had joined Chicano and Chicana students in the Third World Student Strike in 1969. They demanded that U.C. reach out to the communities in California, specifically to recruit students of color as special admissions and to establish a Third World College. While I worked on campus, I almost never saw Guillermo there. He wanted to keep his family life separate from his campus life.

Six months later, I got a job working for Professor J. Oswaldo Asturias, who headed the Latino Project. The project was an internship program for bilingual teachers in the Mission District, with its main office on the U.C. campus. Months later, by "a flip of a coin" between him and Dr. Octavio Romano, Professor Asturias became the first coordinator of La Raza Studies, afterwards renamed Chicano Studies. By an extension of duties, I became the "unofficial" secretary of Chicano Studies, taking care of all the paperwork to hire new faculty, order supplies, to see to other program needs and to train the secretary when she was finally hired.

It should have been obvious to Guillermo and me that we were growing emotionally distant from each other. Neither of us realized then that the fabric of our life together had begun to fray and would soon be torn apart beyond repair. By late fall in 1969, I had moved out of the flat on Ashby Avenue we shared, taking with me only my son, his and my personal belongings, and my family photos and letters. The creatures in my dreams knew about it long before our physical separation occurred. And *el loco* Andrés' fierce avatar came back full force and, one by one, all of Morpheus' dream terrorists broke through my defenses and seized my dream world once again.

With such an active horde of bold and crazed creatures in my subconscious, and me armed with a reptilian brain determined to keep me safe at all costs, my dreams became battlegrounds. As in the past, I'd suddenly awaken just before my head hit the ground, or in a cold sweat, whimpering or praying and calling for my mom and dad. There were nights when my reality was worse than my nightmares, and all I could do was cry, uncertain of my son's future and mine. I had very few friends in whom to confide. I was deeply wounded, and I felt betrayed and forsaken.

In San Luis Potosí, my dad had been diagnosed with stomach cancer. In my dire financial situation, I couldn't come up with the air fare to go and see him and be with my family. I didn't have the heart to tell my parents—especially my father in his precarious health condition—that Guillermo and I had separated, that he had found someone new to love. Ironically, I had no other friends but the creatures in my dreams, scaring me out of my wits. And for the first time, I found comfort in that realization and welcomed their intrusion in my life.

Knowing that it was of utmost importance for me to have a career, I decided to go back to school. I applied for and was admitted to U.C. Berkeley as a sophomore through regular admission, which meant I was only eligible for student loans, including a ten-percent tuition deferment, which I would also have to pay back. Working thirty hours a week and carrying twelve academic units was hard, to say the least. One third of my salary was going into paying for the nursery school Arturo was attending by then, and twenty-five percent into rent. Although I managed to put aside some dollars in a contingency savings account by robbing my entertainment, wardrobe and shoe funds, the remainder went to cover the rest of my monthly expenses, including my tuition, books and supplies.

Unable to get to sleep after studying hard for a test one night, I reached for paper and pencil simply to give voice to my pain and my questions, to examine my contradictions and the avenues open to me and my son. At first, the writing was obscure and nightmarish. I was sure Morpheus and his band of dream terrorists guided my hand now in vigil, just as they had taken over my psyche in slumber. But every night I felt at peace. The bits of joy I experienced as I wrote, however, were not enough to keep me from plummeting to the ground. I still woke up with a start and a sigh of relief. Like Scheherazade, every night, on my word, I earned the right to live yet another day.

In Mexico, my dad's cancer had metastasized to the pancreas, which much sooner than later would take his life. Finally, Arturo and I were able to travel to San Luis to see him and spend two weeks with him and the rest of my family. I hid my tears from him and let him see only my smiles. I was grateful to be with him, see him enjoy Arturo's company. It would be the last time I enjoyed his company, his laughter and amusing stories, his music. Most of all, I would miss his loving, reassuring embrace. Weak as he was, he insisted on going to the bus depot to see us off to Mexico City, where we were to board the plane back to San Francisco. My father stood very still on the platform as we stepped up into the bus. I found and took our seats quickly so I could hold him in my gaze for as long as possible and etch his image in my memory. As the bus backed out, then started out of the yard, he smiled. He reached for and took off his trademark hat and placed it on his chest near his heart as a sign of his love and respect for us. It would be impossible for Arturo and me to go back for his funeral. For the rest of my life, this would be the image I would come back to every day as I thought of him, and as I tried to honor him by striving to do and to be the best I could, as he had taught me. In his memory, I wrote every night.

Writing gave me the strength to go on one day at a time. It provided me with the certainty and reassurance I badly needed. Like everything good and bad in my life, this dark period of emotional wants and financial woes—my lean years—would also come to an end one day. Arturo and I would make it. Gradually, my writing began to transform into verses I threaded into short lyrics then longer poems in Spanish. My spirit soared in my dreams, but I no longer fell toward the ground. For the next ten years, I wrote every night, certain that if I stopped writing I would literally wither away and die.

During that decade, I had no dreams, and if I did, they burned up in the light of reality. It would take me two years to call what I wrote poetry or call myself a poet. Despite the problems I encountered, or the times that nostalgia and loneliness threatened to overpower me, I always looked forward to my late-night writing sessions. Nothing I did before that time made me feel as complete as writing. I was in a space entirely my own. One night, after finishing a series of four poems I titled "The Marina Poems," I finally acknowledged that I had been born to be a poet, and that poetry had held the power to conquer mighty Morpheus and his dream terrorists. By then I had graduated from Cal and moved to Oakland, where I had gotten my first job as a teacher in the Oakland Public Schools' adult education program.

After ten years of writing poetry every night, for no comprehensible reason, words swung in the whirlwinds of my mind but did not fall to fertile ground to take root. My hand could no longer record on paper the interplay of the conscious with the subconscious and the subliminal elements that came together to give the poem's internal rhythms their measure and tone. I could no longer grasp and make mine the imagery or the storyline in it, or to construct the structure that supported the poem's emotional weight.

I had no idea that these lulls in the creative process were natural. In my case, there were three areas that demanded the best of my creativity: parenthood, teaching and writing. Creative energy does not spring from a bottomless well. When the demand upon one's creativity is excessive, the well dries up for awhile. So mine had to be replenished about then. Nonetheless, while going through it, I was terrified by the possibility that I would never write another poem. Soon after, and for the next two years, the nightmares took possession of my nights again.

Terrific, although enigmatic, were the recurring death dreams within a dream, which I classified as "catatonic" for lack of a better word. A man sometimes, but frequently a woman, wearing white clothes, laid in an open grave, or in a mausoleum in the midst of a forest, at night or midday. "What am I doing here?" The first time I voiced that question, the realization that I was actually the stranger in the grave or trapped in the mausoleum filled me with a kind of panic as yet unknown to me. I would seemingly come-to only to find out I was still caught in the dream web, unable to extricate myself from it and really wake up. After what seemed an eternity of unmitigated terror, I would manage to wake up, gasping for breath but relieved to still be alive.

My anxiety began to manifest itself physically as painful stomach cramps that interrupted sleep and that only cold milk or ice cream could soothe. I also suffered from a heartburn that limited my diet to bland foods, well-cooked meats, poultry and vegetables. Even that was not enough to stave off the pain, and when it became intolerable, I went to the doctor. What I already suspected was confirmed: I had developed a stomach ulcer and had to undergo treatment for it. In addition to taking daily medication and watching my diet, I also attended a series of sessions at the bio-feedback clinic. They helped me to identify the kinds of stress that were causing such anxiety in me. I could then learn to modify my response to those particular stressful situations. During the initial interview, I was asked to identify those activities that made me relax and have fun, and those that caused me to stress out. My own observations along the years proved to be true. Writing, reading, swimming, going for walks on the beach or to picnics with my son or good friends, watching movies topped the list. No matter the problems, teaching was thoroughly satisfying and there wasn't a day that I didn't look forward to it. Stressful were the situations where I had no way to know, let alone control, the unforeseen circumstances and factors in them so I could prepare for their impact. That was the unknown that Morpheus had been preparing me for all those years. My underworld god and his progeny had been trying to teach me patience, persistence, not tolerance but acceptance, and knowing how to let go when there was nothing to be done about a situation.

To pass the time I had devoted to poetry before and in hopes that any kind of writing would speed up the healing of my ulcer, I began to write short stories in Spanish. Writing a short story could take several weeks. It would be followed by a lull, a kind of gestation period needed to bring all the elements in the next story together in my mind. Whether I produced anything worth the effort or not, I faithfully sat at my writing table every night, hoping that being so bored would make me want to write to keep myself entertained. Most of the time, my plan worked.

One winter night, exhausted and unable to get any ideas, I fell asleep, pen in hand, head resting on the ruled paper tablet on the table. At some point, I acknowledged the sound of softly falling rain outside my window, which at other times would have awakened me. Instead, I blended the element of the murmuring rain into a fluid dream that had begun to take shape in me. A man and a woman swam in calm water. Suddenly a storm raged, and they began to swim toward an oar boat that kept drifting farther and farther away from them. I knew they were in trouble. I acknowledged that the man was my beloved husband, and the woman, my dear cousin and friend. I was certain that they were falling in love with one another, and just as surely that I could only save one of them. As I watched them go under, I swam to the spot where I had last seen them. As I dove down, I was totally convinced that I would save him, the husband who had already forsaken me. "Playing God?" I heard myself ask in the dream. I woke up with the heavy load of guilt and grief pressing against my heart and lungs.

The dream scene and the overwhelming feelings it produced in me tainted everything I did that day. I could not make any sense of it. Sitting at my writing table that evening, late, I suspected that the dream had to do with a lot more than my present circumstances and my illness. So I began to write it up, as always in Spanish. Then I realized that the cries for help that alerted me to someone at peril in the water had been in English, not Spanish. I had been aware before that I could dream in any or both my languages. As I went on putting my dream down on paper, the voices in it began to speak to me in English only. The first-person narrative I wrote was in the voice of Eva, the wife, who had chosen to save her husband instead of her cousin.

When I finished the story, "Shadows on Ebbing Water," I was elated to discover that I could put Morpheus's dreams to good use. Nevertheless, I was intrigued by a sensation of incompleteness, as if my spirit had been split and I was unable to mend it back together. For awhile, I didn't write and I didn't dream. Luckily, just as it had suddenly and mysteriously flown away, my poetry came back. But my voice had changed. Its tone was somber; its light and color dimmer as one finds in interior settings. Despite this development, I immediately felt mended and healed. I felt complete again.

One night, just before waking up, I dreamt of fire. A circle of flames surrounded me—yellow at first, then red, then blinding white and black and finally green. I wasn't afraid, but rather fascinated. A moment later, I walked through and out of the circle of fire unscathed. A small single-room structure with a door rose next to it. I couldn't bring myself to open the door and walk in. I promised myself that I would open that door and face my fear, the unknown behind it, if I had that dream again. As I'd done before, I wrote the fire dream and it soon evolved into another much longer story than the previous one, and the characters also communicated in English. The protagonist's name was Delia, so I gave it a working title, "Delia's Song." Every time I trimmed something, like a plant, it grew in other places.

Frustrated, I sought the help of my good friend, the novelist Margaret Shedd, founder of El Centro Mexicano de Escritores—The Mexican Center for Writers—in the 50s in Mexico City, and of the Chicano arts service organization Aztlán Cultural in Berkeley in the 70s. She had invited me to be a board member of the organization, and I'd accepted. I asked her to read my story and give me an idea how or where to trim it. Margaret and I met two weeks later. "This is no longer a short story," she told me. "What you have here are the first two or three chapters of a novel." When she saw the expression of disbelief, then dismay on my face, she gave me an ample smile and said: "See you in two years."

Panic set in. I wasn't ready to devote the time and effort it would take me to write a lengthier work, let alone in English, my second language. It would test me in ways I hadn't been and wasn't ready to be tested. I shelved the story and tried to put it out of my mind, but the urge I felt to retrieve it and work on it wouldn't let up, and after a year, I finally decided to commit to it, come what may. My goal for *Delia's Song* was to alternately contrast narrative and first-person voices throughout the novel.

The first-person voice took the form of interior monologue. To be able to write it, I had to experience or sense and acknowledge the stream of consciousness process. I had to identify its possible source or sources and the way it was controlled by the unconscious mind. Using myself as a mental lab rat, countless times, with my eyes open, I sat in silence and stillness but purposely aware of the various levels of consciousness in me. At other times, I concentrated on the messages my body was sending to my mind. Also, what my conscious mind did with the information collected, and how stimuli manifested themselves through my five senses and in turn affected my conscious mind.

The creative process brought to the forefront all the ways in which I lacked the fluidity and richness of language and the cultural knowledge the story demanded from me. But I was determined to get it done, and in many ways, I found the challenges invigorating. My narrative voice in English had not interfered with the lyrical voice in Spanish, and thus far I had been able to write both poetry and story, each in their separate worlds. I didn't feel split or unable to handle the unforeseeable or unknown elements writing in two languages might have created. So there were no nightmares to speak of during those years. Actually, Morpheus and his band of dream voyeurs seemed to be rewarding me with my own sex fantasy dreams, as I wrote about Delia's emotional escapes from reality and her sexual escapades. Some of mine were actually amusing in the light of day. I ventured the assumption that Morpheus and his band kept watch on me from the sidelines. They would remain there only as long as my bicultural, bilingual selves provided one another with the ballast to stay their individual courses.

One of the fantasy dreams in particular caught my attention, not so much as a sex fantasy but as a way to explore the Morpheus persona in me. I was in the back of a limo necking with Bill Bixby and getting ready to go all the way. Bixby was the actor that had played the role of Dr. Bruce Banner in the original TV series "The Incredible Hulk." Basically, it was a

Dr. Jekyll and Mr. Hyde story, but with a twist. In an odd way, the Hulk became a crusader for justice. I had watched every episode, and I had empathized with Bruce Banner's tragic condition that allowed the angry monster in him—the creation— to control the scientist—the creator. The fact was that I had never found Bixby physically attractive. Yet, there was I, in the back of the limo in hot embrace with a man who could turn into a violent, glowing green monster at the snap of anyone's angry fingers. Kin-n-ky! Unlike Hyde, however, Hulk wasn't entirely an evil alter ego. In their delicately balanced symbiotic relationship, Banner and Hulk had influence over one another. Hulk shared in Banner's desire for justice, since he strictly meted his kind of justice out to those who perpetrated evil.

I realized that my relationship with Morpheus had also become a symbiotic relationship over a thirty-year span. It had grown beyond classifying the strong emotions, feelings and experiences that triggered some dreadful dreams. In most instances, I had already identified fear as the most powerful of them. Fear of the unknown. Fear that ensured my survival by testing my resolve and strength to overcome any difficult situation I faced or life would pit me against. Now I also had to acknowledge that my purposeful delving into the various levels from subliminal to subconscious to conscious and vice versa as I wrote the novel, had changed my perspective. It had influenced the way I felt and thought about my nightmares. It was then that I began to distinguish between random nightmares coming from the depths of my unconscious, and those dreams that were produced through collaboration between my subconscious and conscious selves, which in turn benefited my writing.

I had finished about two thirds of Delia's story when I was confronted with problems in the narrative and a coincidental short pause in the poetry at the same time. Morpheus showed up once again with fire in his hands. I was surrounded by flames again, but this time I knew I would get burned if I stayed within the narrowing circle. My only escape from it was opening the door and walking into the small one-room structure next to the rim of fire. As I went through the portal of my dream and stepped into the dim light of the room, I had regressed to an early age and sensed the presence of a man awaiting me. A flash of white light struck my eyes. Then I saw the shining blade in his hand. He stuck his hand in my mouth and pulled out my tongue, and with a swift movement slashed it off. I didn't feel pain. Rather I wanted to ask him why he had taken my voice away, what I had done to deserve being silenced. But I couldn't, as I no longer had a tongue. I was overtaken by panic as I felt my hot blood running down my chest. My victimizer dropped the blade and reached for me as if to embrace me. As I withdrew through the open door stepping back into the rim of fire, I suddenly awoke with an aching, inflamed throat. In the darkness, I reached into my mouth to make sure that my tongue was still intact.

Stunned, I was unable to deal with the possibility that I had a desire to punish myself, to destroy the instrument of voice in me—my writing voice, the only virtue that defined me and made me feel complete in ways that nothing else did! This was it! I had reached the end of my patience with Morpheus and the dream terrorists. In the newspaper, I had seen an ad for a psychologist who specialized in dream therapy, but when I called his office, I found out the cost of even one session was prohibitive for me. And my case was going to require quite a few sessions, I was sure. Armed with my list of questions, I went to the place where the two most outstanding psychiatrists dwelled, the place where I could find the many answers I needed: the Oakland Public Library. There in black and white I met Carl Jung, a friend and mentee of Freud's, and with whom I spent many a lunch hour for weeks.

I had read Freud's *Civilization and Its Discontents* for a class at Cal. It was an illuminating book for me. It dealt with philosophical and psychological questions about daily existence, about the individual human being within and apart from society. Freud saw the roles of religion and the legal system as attempts to guide every man as he navigated the locks between his instinct for love and the drive to destroy. Both systems were supposed to help him transcend thus survive his own wild nature, to control the drive to destroy it all, including himself and his own creations—the death drive. I found *Civilization* a fascinating read, especially because at the time I was also reading *The Odyssey* for a class and somehow, to my way of reading him, Odysseus was that everyman. I would think about Freud's and Homer's works many years later, while laboring day after day to read James Joyce's *Ulysses*.

Eager to read Freud's *Interpretation of Dreams*, I chose what turned out to be a dense and difficult translation of it. I ploughed through the book till the end. I agreed that as human beings we all, men and women, had dreams that followed certain insidious patterns across sexes and cultures. They could be classified as belonging to this or that universal category. I, however, questioned whether having the subconscious, the ego and self of a woman made a difference. I was conditioned by society at large to think that I belonged to the weaker sex. I had been told that I was guided entirely by my feelings and emotions not my intellect. I had even considered it true that my life had to be lived exclusively in service to others. I was mistaken to think that all of these things constituted the best in me and had a great deal to do with the kind of day or night dreams I dreamt.

My own perspective on things was different from Freud's. I was a thinking and feeling woman and I had learned to use and trust my instincts and intuition. I had made decisions backed by my own convictions and beliefs. I had accepted responsibility for the consequences of my actions. Freud's set of values, imposed on me by males, did not even begin to define who I was.

Carl Jung, who Freud had mentored, had a different approach to the analysis of dreams, and his style of writing made his work more accessible even in translation. I first read Jung's *Man and His Symbols*. Although his was still a male-centered analysis, his notion of "individuation" in the analysis of dreams and other experiences served me well. Distilling his theories into a more personal pool of experience, I realized that I could not hope to understand the human psyche in all its aspects, and mine in particular, without taking into consideration the only possible context for it: the entire self, shared by the ego, the animus (the male aspect) and the anima (the female aspect) present in each human being, as Jung proposed. Framing my latest nightmare in that kind of analysis, it seemed logical to me that the animus, the public persona, wanted me silent while the other, the private anima, was quite willing to self-sacrifice. I had the feeling that something was out of kilter in this framework, and until I found out what it was, it seemed useless to pursue the writing of *Delia's Song*.

By coincidence, I met Norma Alarcón at that time. She was a post-doctoral fellow at Berkeley for a year, but later applied and was hired for a position as professor at U.C. Berkeley's Chicano Studies. I happened to learn that a flat across from my home had become available for rent and I let her know about it. She and her husband moved in across the street from me. We saw each other often and enjoyed talking. Gradually our friendship got solidified. On one occasion, our conversation turned to the subject of journal writing. She told me she had kept a journal of her dreams for a long time. She remembered her dreams clearly and every morning she wrote them down in her dream journal, for later review as to their significance. She asked me if I remembered my dreams. I had learned to trust her, I decided to tell her about my most terrible nightmares. I couldn't keep a diary of nightmares when all I had ever wanted was to forget them. I could see in her eyes her disbelief but not rejection. She explained that it was difficult for her to believe that I had such violent dreams. I seemed, and she was sure, I was even-tempered and pretty much in control of my life. That was the first of many talks about dreams we had. I learned to trust her with my deepest secrets, my dreams.

The desire to explore my nightmares and use them to feed my writing was renewed through my friendship with Norma. I went back to the tongue-slicing nightmare, but I was still unable to determine what my doubts were or what that missing balancing factor was that had made me stop writing. I then decided to go back to the only thing that made everything all right for me: writing. I lost myself in the world of Delia's story. Late one night, I finished the chapter I was working and didn't want to start a new one. I went to bed and must have been asleep a couple of hours when I awoke with an extreme urge to go back to the novel. Lo and behold, the first thing I wrote was a version of the sliced-tongue nightmare in my character Delia's words. I was stunned to see it was actually Delia's experience, not mine, I had dreamt. I did not question the process that had taken me there, but took it at face value, and began to trust that my dreams were those of a writer or a poet. For the first time in thirty years, I welcomed them without reservations.

My trust in Morpheus and his mind-controlling progeny had prepared me for the extrasensory visions of my Chicana detective Gloria Damasco, who came to me in dreams, and for the nightmares experienced by other characters in my novels. I learned to identify the dreams as theirs when that was the case. In one dream, I was walking through a series of dimly lit underground tunnels. Turning a corner, I found myself facing a gun. Without warning, the hand holding it pulled the trigger and shot me in the forehead. Writing my crime novel *Crimson Moon*, I realized that the dream belonged to my male detective Justin Escobar. In still another dream, I found myself struggling to swim up to the surface and gasping for breath as I tried to stay afloat. It turned out to be one of Gloria's visions and later her desperate effort to save a child and his mother trapped in a car at the bottom of a lake in the fictitious reality of my novel *Death at Solstice*.

Sixty years later, my dream world is still populated by nightmares and other kinds of dreams made possible by the madman Andrés, for whom I now feel nothing but compassion and gratitude. Without him, the flood gates of my unconscious and subconscious would have remained locked inside me, and Morpheus and his progeny would have remained prisoners in the dark dungeons of my mind. Instead, it is because of all of them that I found and continue to find the courage to face my fears and my unknowns, and to discover in myself the images, symbols, music, intuitions and so many other things that go into each poem or story. In the end, all of them have given me the greatest rewards I have ever received: the gifts of poetry and narrative and the courage to do their writing regardless of circumstance.

WINGS, CHIMES AND LAUREL WREATHS: MISSING DESTINY

Destiny: A tyrant's authority for crime and a fool's excuse for failure.

—Ambrose Bierce

Canción de Invierno / Winter Song

Cantando baja la lluvia	*The rain comes down singing*
a su destino de mineral y semilla.	*toward its destiny of mineral and seed.*
Entre el hueco del ala que se extiende	*Between the hollow of an opening wing*
y el entrecerrar de la mirada que descansa	*and the lowering of eyelids in repose*
aprendemos a amar en instantes y entregas	*we learn to love in instants and surrenders*
y entre la pregunta íntima de la	*and between the intimate question posed*
noche	*by night*
y la respuesta dulciobscura de la madrugada	*and the darksweet reply given by dawn*
gestamos dolorosamente una nueva vida.	*we engender in pain a new life.*
Nada hay fijo ni perenne	*Nothing is fixed or perpetual*
ni la lluvia	*not rain*
ni la semilla	*or seed*
ni tú	*or you*
ni yo	*or I*
ni nuestro dolor	*or our grief*
en este mundo que sangra	*in this world that is bleeding*
porque vamos siempre tirando senda	*because we're forever cutting paths*
abriendo brecha por caminos desconocidos	*opening our way along unfamiliar roads*
venciendo la furia del olvido verso a verso.	*conquering the fury of oblivion verse by verse.*

English translation by Catherine Rodríguez-Nieto

WHEN I FIRST HEARD THE WORD DESTINY, I was almost six years old.

"*Era su destino morir joven*—It was her destiny to die young," someone said at a burial and sighed.

"Is death my destiny?" I asked anyone who'd listen.

"We will all die one day," my brother's godmother said.

"It's a game of hide-and-seek. You hide and death finds you. That's all," my older brother Víctor replied. I could always count on his matter-of-factness.

"Destiny is just another word for life, your life. No one else's," my mother explained, as she dipped a dead chicken, head first, in a pot of boiling water so we could easily pluck off the feathers and peel his legs and feet.

"Destiny must be a good thing, like good luck," my best friend Marta said as she mounted her brother Paco's bike.

"I don't believe that. Destiny killed that lady. She was very young," I argued, but Marta was already pedaling away. She was always in a hurry to go somewhere, anywhere.

At home, I asked my father. He turned down the radio volume. With a wink and a smile he answered, "You are you and your own destiny." I didn't know exactly what his answer meant. But it felt good to be important enough to be me and my own destiny.

"Only God knows. Your destiny and mine and everyone else's fate are already written in God's Book of Life," our parish priest said, lighting a votive candle and making the sign of the cross.

I'd already done my share of handwriting and copying of school material. God had all of my sympathy. The enormity of his task, just in writing the name and destiny of each one in our village in Veracruz, more than two thousand of us, was something beyond my comprehension, like trying to count hairs in braids or tallying the total of restless fireflies. "*Pobrecito Dios*," I thought.

"But may I read God's book?" I asked the priest. He upturned a brow and went on to look after other less inquisitive parishioners.

I finally asked Abuelita Nico, my grandmother, and she answered: "It's who you were meant to be and what you were born to do in life. But destiny won't find you. You have to go and find yours."

Perhaps San Luis Potosí, where my family had relocated in the winter of 1953, was a stop on the road to my destiny. For all the good reasons given to us children—a better job for my father, better schools for us, more money at home, a healthier climate—moving to San Luis had been entirely my parents' decision, not my siblings' or my choice. My reason for being on this earth seemed to be tied to the destiny of my entire family. I imagined us as a Mexican lace cloth, made of individual pieces crocheted together in such a way that each piece could be separated from the rest when the time came. Maybe I had to be older, of age, to earn the right to find the reason for my existence. I was willing to wait as long as it took to find it.

At age fourteen, destiny had become more than an enigmatic or exotic word. In the form of an adage, a fable or a personal comment, people expressed their own views of what it personally meant to them. And these views were more than often extreme in their positivity (destiny) or negativity (fate). Like the anodes and cathodes of human existence, fate and destiny seemed to tug at and repel each other's energies to keep life on an even keel and thriving. And I began to understand the emotional charge held by each set of terms used to describe this force: destiny and fate, fortune and misfortune, recompense and retribution, synchronicity and serendipity.

The priest of my childhood had told me that somewhere in Heaven there was a book written exclusively for me, the blueprint for my life. But I still wasn't any closer to understanding or finding my own destiny than at age six, when the concept and lore about it had first captivated me. I had nothing but questions, and no one to help me understand.

I asked Father Fernando, a priest who taught us Ethics and Logic and Greek and Latin Etymology in high school, if the priest of my childhood was right.

"It's been said that all that happens from the beginning of time to the end of days has already been written," he answered.

"That's what the other priest said, but what do *you* think?" I insisted.

"That God also gave us free will. We choose. Even Jesus had to choose. Remember His last temptation? He wanted His Father to spare him."

"And Judas, I don't think he had a choice," I said.

"He certainly did," Father Fernando replied, throwing his shoulders back.

"What would have happened if he hadn't betrayed Jesus?" I asked.

"Another Judas would have taken his place. In life, you can always count on another Judas. And the prophecy would have still been fulfilled."

"I know some people who have the gift of prophecy," I said, curious to hear his take on the subject.

"You mean fortune-telling or magic? Prophecy is a gift from God. No ordinary human can predict the future. Anything like that isn't the work of God. Other dark forces are at work. You know that," he said, and looked at me long until I lowered my eyes.

"But the prophets were ordinary humans, weren't they?" I asked, almost in a whisper.

He put his hand on my shoulder and said, "You're very smart. That's why I like talking with you. Just be sure you're not too smart for your own good. It'll only bring you unhappiness."

It was too late for the warning. I had already begun to question some of the Catholic Church's practices and beliefs, and in two years, I would, of my own volition, stop going to church. The unhappiness my smartness would bring me was also of little concern. At that moment, I was more interested in what Father Fernando had inadvertently let slip out, that the prophecy would have been fulfilled regardless. So destiny was a fixed game. Forget the free will, according to that. Exercising it would be like swimming against the current or pushing a rock up a hill. Yet, more intriguing was the possibility that there was a way to see into the future, regardless of the outcome. Some people like Abuelita Nico and my sister Conchita had the gift of seeing in ways that most of us couldn't.

To my mother's way of thinking during our childhood, if you knew what was going to happen, you could do something to change the outcome or stop fate's dark forces altogether. Mom cringed every time my sister Conchita issued a warning in some sort of codified language that only my mom and I dared to decipher. When we were all young and my sister said, "Marbles, Vitín," my mother ran to hide my brother Víctor's bag of marbles from him. But my brother got hit by a couple of marbles anyway as he watched two other boys hurl them at each other over who'd won a game. It was his fate to come home with a swollen and bruised left brow and lid.

My sister's prophetic visions were full of coded sensory information, which not even she could break and rearrange into meaningful and comprehensible messages. My mom and

I also tried, although often failed, to derive somewhat accurate meaning from the many images, smells, sounds and symbols in her visions. Accurate interpretation was nearly impossible for anyone, including the seer. If by chance, the interpreter was correct, there was really no way to alter the outcome. The whole thing seemed quite unfair and senseless.

From what I'd learned about it until then, destiny was a living, unstoppable force that propelled each of us onto a personal road. Ironically, it seemed to follow always in the wake of those who intently looked for their fate. I used to imagine destiny as a vehicle traveling through the darkest places right behind me, its headlights illuminating the road to my future. But it was up to me to interpret the signs along the way correctly and be at the right place at a precise time.

At night or in my dreams, fate was an ominous figure, a guardian angel, or the angel of death perhaps, a messenger with warnings and omens. However, since there was no way to alter the future, even when one knew what was coming, exercising my free will seemed to be the only possibility for a life lived on my own terms and under my control. Deep inside, nonetheless, I suspected that if fate was inexorable, it would sooner or later catch up to me, no matter the many detours from my main road I might take.

In 1961, at age sixteen, I graduated from high school as expected. I entered dentistry school to please my parents, and I met Guillermo Hernández-Stevens, the man I would eventually marry. In 1964, at age nineteen, of my own free will, I left dentistry school, then married Guillermo and traveled with him to Berkeley, California, where my destiny, once again, caught up to me five years later.

After a painful divorce at age 24, I began to look more closely at the threads in destiny's fabric, but I still had more questions than answers. It seemed clearer that some people "happened" in our lives, whose sole purpose was to serve as "vehicles" to deliver us to our destiny. To date, I believe Guillermo happened in my life for that particular reason. We had a wonderful child together, and that was reason enough to be grateful for our union. Through my relationship with Guillermo, I had grown intellectually by leaps and bounds; I had also rediscovered literature and philosophy. I am not sure how I too impacted his life or thought, but it was evident I had not been meant for him.

Perhaps I had not been meant to be a married woman at all, nor had I been meant to leave my country. Yet I was almost sure that I would have inevitably left Mexico and traveled to another country, perhaps France, Greece or Italy. Coming to the United States had never entered my mind. So I took French and not English as my foreign language in high school. Still, I couldn't help marvel at the possibility that Berkeley was a stop on the road that led to the reason for my existence.

After my divorce in 1970, I was faced with the possibility that I might spend the rest of my life far away from everything I had ever known and everyone who cared what happened to me. The San Francisco Bay Area was full of exciting cities, some that bore Spanish names, as California had once been part of Mexico. But these places were a part of a world alien to me. Even after five years of speaking English, my face and throat muscles ached at night from the effort to utter the right sounds. I had no family in Berkeley and very few friends. I did have a very young son to bring up. His whole well-being and future, and mine, rested mostly on my shoulders.

I wrestled with the pros and cons of going back home, to Mexico, a ninety-nine-percent Catholic country at the time, where a divorced woman was an irreparable tear in the social fabric, where my son might be made to pay for the "sins" of his parents. I would have to live under the auspices of my parents again, when I was already a parent myself. Fate or destiny or none, I decided to stay in the Bay Area and make a life with my son there, knowing that my heart would always be split in two, for mine was in part the story common to all immigrants.

Migration to and assimilation into another culture is a fluid process, like the waters of a delta or estuary fed by two powerful yet distinct, if not opposite, currents. No matter the country of origin or adoption, all of us immigrants for the rest of our lives have to straddle two cultures and learn to feel and think in their respective linguistic systems. Some commonly shared bicultural principles and values thrive. Daily rituals, social customs, family practices and gender roles require constant revision and re-negotiating. Religious and political beliefs, even when shared by both sociocultural systems, often become adversarial more than conciliatory in practice. One thing seemed certain to me at the time of my divorce, that I was facing a life alone, as a single mother, for I had no intention of ever remarrying.

To express my contradictions and my loneliness, to work out the deep sadness and the feelings of abandonment that welled in me, I began to write poetry. Although it would take a couple of years for me to call what I wrote poetry, and three to call myself a poet, nothing before then had made me feel so complete. Writing poetry made it possible for me to move beyond the personal and to transcend my predicaments and vicissitudes in the process. No wants went unfulfilled. The world worked, and I too within it. And I discovered that my grandmother was right. Whatever else my destiny held for me or I chose to do, writing poetry and later narrative was what I'd been born to do in this life. I surrendered to it, as if to a lover, every night, late, for the next ten years.

Destiny and I faced off again in 1980, when I was 35. I had just won a National Endowment for the Arts poetry fellowship. For once in my life, I had a chance to travel and promote my work. I wanted to explore the possibility of being represented in the Spanish-speaking world by a major literary agency in Barcelona. I had also accepted an invitation from American Studies Professor Wolfgang Binder to present my work in Erlangen, West Germany.

On the eve of my departure, I was writing a letter-poem to my son Arturo. He was spending the summer with my cousin Dulce María and her family in my hometown in Mexico while I traveled. The phone rang and I knew it was my sister Conchita. As a rule, we called each other late at night, when preparations for the next day were done, both our kitchens were clean, our children asleep and our homes quiet. It was then we exchanged news in whispers and laughed softly, just like when we were very young girls and shared the same room. So when I picked up the receiver and Conchita's first words were "*Te vi*—I saw you," I got my notebook and pencil ready.

"What was I doing when you saw me?" I asked, knowing that for the next half hour or so we would both try to decipher the code or make sense of the cryptic sensory images in her visions.

"I hear the flapping of wings and the ticking of what I think is a metronome, like the one we used when we practiced the piano. There's a scent of laurel leaves. I see light reflected on metal, shining like when light hits gold. I see a road sign, a word written on it. I can't see the name of the city clearly but I sense it is Vienna. Are you planning to go to Vienna?"

"I am. Maybe that's what the metronome means—the music, you know. Schubert, Strauss. Probably the wings are those of an eagle. The eagle is a symbol of royalty in many European cities. Laurel trees are everywhere around the Mediterranean Sea, but maybe in Vienna, too. Who knows? Gold must mean some kind of jewelry."

My sister was quiet for a while. Something was obviously bothering her. I braced my heart in case it was bad news.

"Tell me the rest, Manita—Sis." No word out of her. "Would you please just tell me," I insisted. "What's going to happen to me there?"

"When you find all these things in one place, you'll see a man. His name is Jean Philippe. He is the man meant for you, your destiny. He's about medium height, thin, very light brown hair, almost blond. He's wearing a dark gray suit, a light blue shirt and a dark blue necktie."

It was the first time my sister had described someone in great detail. This rendezvous with my destiny-man was serious business. The prospect filled me with anxiety.

I visited a few European cities before I arrived in Vienna, on my way to Nuremberg-Erlangen in Germany, my final destination before returning home. The anticipation of meeting this Jean Philippe grew as I got closer to Austria. The voice of caution every so often reminded me that the man I was destined for lived ten thousand miles away from everything I knew and held dear. *I was destined for* . . . the words bounced back from a mental wall. I'd believed that my former husband had been meant for me. But obviously I hadn't been for him. What if this Viennese man was part of my destiny but I not of his? Although when I was younger, I had acknowledged that reciprocity and synchronicity had something to do with finding your destiny, I hadn't considered how truly necessary both factors were for destiny's enterprises to succeed.

It was raining when I finally arrived in Franz Schubert's birth place. No doubt, Vienna was a beautiful city and perhaps more so in stormy weather. Somewhere between Venice and Vienna I had caught a cold, and my energy had dwindled. Yet I forced myself to go out that evening and the next day. I looked for eagles on interior and exterior walls and staircases of buildings, and on monuments. I found none. Nor did I see the green of laurel trees in parks, gardens and city sidewalks, or the peculiar dazzling brilliance of gold my sister had described. The sound of metronomes was perhaps drowned by the steady whoosh of cascading rain. The man in the gray suit and blue shirt eluded me during two infinitely gray and melancholic days.

On the third day, feeling physically and emotionally spent, I got to my hotel in the late afternoon. Foregoing dinner, I went to bed and slept. Voices outside my room woke me up, but they faded as hotel guests walked down the hall to their rooms. My whole body shook, seized by chills. I was more ill than anticipated. Hot tears rolled down my face, making the wall of the dam in my nose break and its content run freely. I wasn't sure why I cried. As I reached for a tissue on the night stand to blow my nose, I heard a distant single bell stroke. With eyes open to the dark, I felt fear's tentacles squeeze my heart, making my breathing even thinner. I was thousands of miles away from home, from my son enjoying the summer in Mexico. I was alone, sick, and in a city where destiny wore a gray suit but had remained a stranger. I cried myself to sleep.

I went downstairs for breakfast but could only tolerate hot tea with lots of lemon juice and honey. I overheard a couple at the next table, American tourists, planning to take the train to Lucerne in Switzerland to get away from the dreariness of Vienna. It was sunny there, and warm, and the views were magnificent. Without further delay or hesitation, I went upstairs, quickly packed my one, very large suitcase, in which I was sure my small body could snuggly fit. Shaking off that dreadful image that sent chills up my spine, I lugged my bag to the elevator. The clerk at the front desk recommended a hotel in Lucerne. Although it occurred to me that running away from my destiny might be of grave consequence, I was too sick to regret my decision then.

Minutes after settling in my seat on the train, I went to sleep. When I opened my eyes again, I was being asked for my ticket and documents. Sloping green kept me company all the way to Lucerne, where I arrived in the early evening. By the time I got to the hotel, I was beginning to feel better. Luckily, there was a single room available. The next morning, I was awakened by the pealing of church bells. It was Sunday morning. Feeling more cheerful and healthier than I had in days, I decided to get a watch for my son. No better place for it than Switzerland, the land of the precision timepiece. The trick was to find a store that sold watches open on Sunday. Most retail stores and other business establishments were closed on the seventh day of the week, a day of rest. But luck was on my side. The front desk clerk told me about a store on the other side of the lake. Both the very old, wooden Chapel Bridge or the modern concrete bridge connected to the plaza where the establishment was located. Walking there would be easy and pleasant enough. The store opened at 11 a.m. and at exactly 1 p.m., all customers were asked to leave, I was informed at the hotel, whether they had completed their transactions or not. No exceptions.

At 10 o'clock on that sunny Sunday morning in August, I crossed the old wooden bridge. Upon reaching the other side, I saw the more modern bridge and walked to it. Black and white swans waded in the water, spreading their wings from time to time, as if to say hello or wave goodbye. Cruise ferries full of tourists chugged up stream. Families, dressed in their Sunday best, strolled along the lake shore. I followed their comings and goings while I had coffee and pastry at a sidewalk café across the lake. As I watched the solemn and still white-capped Alps in the distance, I was suddenly aware that I had begun breathing through my nose again.

I headed back to the plaza where the jewelry and watch store was located. Mostly English-speaking tourists gathered there, chatting with one another and checking their watches every so often. I did some window shopping to pass the time and work out a sudden burst of energy.

The whole area teemed with people. Everyone stood literally elbow to elbow on the sidewalk and on a large wedge of concrete that served as a divider between streets. A bunch of tourists began to queue up outside the store doors. As if on cue, people stopped their milling around. A clock behind me chimed in the first of eleven strokes. Craning my neck, I glanced at the clock at the same time that the honking of the swans reached my ears. They sounded nearer, and I raised my eyes again as if expecting to see the large birds fly above us.

I caught sight of the concrete wedge between me and the street at the other end. A short while earlier, people had constantly and restlessly waited there to cross the street. At the moment, only a handful of tourists stood there, among them a man who caught my attention immediately. He stood alone in the center of the place, his arms crossed over his chest, his eyes fixed on something in front of him—behind me. His hair was blond, and he wore a dark gray suit, a light blue shirt and a dark tie.

My breath gushed out of my lungs. My heart seemed bent on squeezing hundreds of beats between clock chimes. I turned around and looked at the building behind me. Above the large front door and windows were stone garlands and wreaths of what seemed to be laurel leaves. I could have sworn that an angel stroked the bell in the clock tower, and another held a crown. Nothing was clear in the glaring light of morning. All I knew, as the last stroke of the eleventh hour rang, was that I had just entered my sister's vision. I was about to step into destiny's cosmic space.

Conflicting voices within me either prompted me to approach the man or warned that he was a stranger and could be a rapist or a murderer. What would happen to my thirteen-year-old son if, instead of my destiny, this stranger was my final destination? Would I have the right to uproot my son and take him so far away from his father and both our families? Was I considering his destiny as well as mine? And if I died so far away from home, who would make sure I was buried in my hometown in Veracruz?

I backed up a few steps in the direction of the store doors, then recovered them, and stepped back then forth again, looking like a clumsy, crazed, midget-size mime, attempting Michael Jackson's moonwalk. My eyes were fixed on the face of the man across the way. "Jean Philippe," was all I had to say, loud and clear. But when I tried to spit the words out, I choked on them. Seized by a coughing spell, I bent forward and covered my mouth with the tissue in my hand. I coughed for no more than five seconds, but by the time I straightened up, most people had walked into the jewelry store, and Jean Philippe, my destiny-man, had also disappeared from sight.

For a few seconds, thoughts dangled incomplete in a mental cellar, like *ristras* of red, half-eaten *chiles*. My stomach felt as if I had indeed eaten most of those peppers. "Dammit! I'm so stupid!!" I crossed my hands over my stomach and pressed and kept cursing under my breath. People tried not to stare, but they definitely steered away from the mad woman panting and talking to herself. The apprehension in their eyes made me get a hold of myself and rethink my next move. I expected to feel regret; instead, I felt relief. But I heard the swans' honking. The wings, the chimes, the laurel wreaths—I had no right to mess with destiny. It was sheer willfulness on my part, and I would pay for it in time, I was sure. I turned around and walked as fast as I could toward the modern concrete bridge. My breathing became again rapid and laborious. My lungs filled with hot air. But I went on.

I finally had the man in sight again. He was standing midway across the bridge, resting his back against the rail. He threw glances left and right, as if he were waiting for someone to meet him there. Turning around, he rested on his elbows and looked down at the water, then let go of something he was holding in his hand. I heard the flapping of wings. The swans below seemed restless. I was facing my moment of truth.

Warnings piled on top of one another in my head, silencing my common sense. Fear gnawed at the little courage left in me. "No, I won't do this—I need time. Besides, if this man is meant for me, and I for him, we will find each other again."

I no longer felt hesitant. For the second time, I headed toward the store. I turned around to have a last look at him. He wasn't anywhere in sight, and this time, I knew I would not look for him. I went into the store. An hour later, I walked out with a very nice watch for my son. I crossed the modern bridge, pausing only for a brief moment to look at the swans from the exact spot Jean Philippe had looked down at them before. The feeling of wellbeing I had experienced earlier that morning had totally dissipated. My feet and hands tingled as if the numbed skin on them struggled to feel again. Then a sudden and fulminating headache made my eyes smart and the skin on my neck, face and scalp itch.

I went into a bistro and ordered a bowl of the soup du jour and a glass of red wine. I drank the wine first, then had half of the hearty soup. Intent on writing down what had just happened, I took my notebook out. Instead, I wrote a short lyric that began with the lines, "*Cantando baja la lluvia /a su destino de mineral y semilla,*" which my great friend and translator,

Catherine Rodríguez-Nieto, later would aptly translate into "The rain comes down singing / toward its destiny of mineral and seed."

The next morning, I headed for Amsterdam. During my journey south to Nuremberg and Erlangen, I finally wrote down the details of my near encounter with my destiny-man. I put my journal aside and tried not to look back to that fateful Sunday in Lucerne. I didn't cry for my loss.

In Erlangen, I kept busy, not a difficult task since I was in the delightful company of my friends and hosts Dr. Wolfgang Binder and José Santiago Morales. They made sure my stay included short trips to neighboring towns. José, who was from Puerto Rico and spoke Spanish and German, was a witty and wonderful host and guide. Wolfgang introduced me to artists, professors, poets and other town folks, who attended my formal presentations as a poet-guest of the city. My time with them was memorably happy.

My two-day trip from Erlangen to Frankfurt to London to San Francisco gave me plenty of time for reflection. No matter how I looked at the facts and the events in Lucerne, they remained the same. My behavior at the plaza and bridge in Lucerne baffled me; not feeling regret didn't. Since I was very young, I had learned to trust my intuition and reason, which alternately served each other's purposes. I believed that walking away had been the right thing to do that first time, and that Jean Philippe and I would meet again. When we did, the outcome would surely be different.

Back in Oakland, a mountain of mail and phone calls to answer kept me occupied and on the move for a couple of days. On the third day, late at night, I called my sister Conchita.

"So, what happened in Vienna?" she immediately asked.

"Nothing, except I got very sick, and the rainy weather didn't help."

"I was wrong," she said.

"I have a present for you," I said, and laughed softly.

She didn't hear me. Her voice dropped down to a whisper. "How could I be so wrong?" she kept asking.

"I didn't say you were wrong. But you need a new cosmic world atlas. And I don't know where I'm going to find one and get it for you, but I will." I chuckled.

"It wasn't Vienna."

"No. It was Lucerne, Switzerland. Black and white swans, a clock on top of a building, not sure but maybe there was an angel with a small hammer striking a bell or maybe holding a crown that reflected an explosion of light. But for sure there was a jewelry and watch store, and a bas-relief of laurel wreaths on one of the buildings. The signs were there, just not in the way or the place we thought."

"Okay. Okay. Did you see Jean Philippe? Did you two meet? What happened?"

Besieged by my sister's constant questions to clarify or explain this or that, I finally finished telling her what had happened that Sunday by Lake Lucerne.

"Next time he and I meet, I promise you that I'll shout his name to all four winds," I said.

I heard my sister's long sigh at the other end. Then, her voice rose at least two decibels. "¡Como eres pendeja, manita!— Boy! Are you an idiot, Sis!"

"What do you mean?" I was a bit miffed.

"You don't understand. There won't be a next time. You missed your chance. You and Jean Phillipe now travel on separate, parallel roads. You won't ever meet again."

Loud sighs at both ends followed. Conchita and I lived two thousand miles from each other, but I could sense her disappointment in me through the wire. Maybe she could also feel my anger rising, not at her but at myself. In all those years, I had been and was still trying to find out what the whole concept of destiny meant. And so far everything had pointed to a series of inexplicable, inexorable, uncontrollable circumstances that would become reality in a person's life, no matter what! It was hard to face that I'd had it all wrong after all those years.

"But isn't it true that there is no way to change destiny?" I tried to argue. "*Que será, será.* What's going to happen will happen regardless of what we do, true?"

"It's not that simple. No one else can change your destiny for you. That's true. But you yourself can. And you had your chance to meet the man destined for you. But you chose not to go along with the program. You'll never meet Jean Philippe again."

"It would have been nice if you'd warned me, right?"

After ten minutes of the blame game, my sister and I made peace with each other and said goodnight. But I was still distraught and unhappy. I pushed back the tears and got in bed. My reason stubbornly refused to let me conciliate sleep. I thought long and hard about the events in Lucerne, my reaction to what happened there and my reluctance to feel any regret whatsoever.

With morning came the acceptance that, no matter what my decision had unleashed, I had no way to change what I'd done. I had taught myself to quickly look at a situation from many angles and make decisions based on reason and conviction, then hope for the best. In this case, I had trusted my intuition and my instinct for survival entirely. Right or wrong, I was ready to live with the consequences.

For the next few days, I wrote every night, inconsequential poems that I burned the next morning. I reviewed the written account in my notebook of the event in Switzerland and tried to find reasons not to believe in what I had written. I tore off the page with the short lyric I had written in Lucerne, and began to work it. It became the middle stanza in "*Canción de Invierno* / Winter Song," a poem that speaks of home, not mine in Oakland but the home of my childhood, and the uncertainties we all face in our own personal lives, regardless of who we are. In it I reaffirm that no matter what lays ahead, poetry is my constant in life; it is the tool or weapon that helps me, every time, to open a new path along new or unfamiliar roads and onto a space entirely my own. Writing the poem is the only way to defeat oblivion, one verse at a time.

I hid the notebook at the bottom of my black trunk, where I kept everything I had ever written. A week later, I picked up my son Arturo at the airport. I showered him with all the presents I had brought for him, including the Swiss watch, which he absolutely loved. Two weeks later we went back to our routines, he to school as a student and I to school as a teacher. I continued writing poetry and stories and knew that as long as I could do that, whatever else my destiny had been and would never again be was no longer of consequence.

Over many years, from time to time, my sister Conchita called at midnight, prefacing our Cinderella chats with a "*te vi*—I saw you," She predicted my second marriage to happen as I entered the seventh cycle of my existence, and she was right. As predicted by her, I was forty-nine when Carlos Medina Gonzales and I got married, a second marriage for both.

Conchita believed that every seven years events happened that lay the foundations for my life-changing experiences. They tested the mettle I was made of, but their impact on my life wasn't evident to me until a few years later. The invaluable lessons learned each time helped me to become a stronger woman, a more accepting human being and a better and humbler poet and fiction writer. She has been right so far.

My sister and I have continued being in contact. But while she was going through a very trying time in her life, Conchita's midnight calls stopped. Then, I called her every Sunday morning, right after I called my mom, knowing how insufferable Sundays can be when someone is going through hard times. When the crisis was over, I continued calling her at different times. However, she never again made predictions about my life, and we never again talked about Jean Philippe or Lucerne. But I've never forgotten that fateful Sunday I let destiny pass me by.

I have worked and reworked that story, as I usually do any real or fictional story. As if it were a batter for a cake or Mexican sweet bread, I add the piquancy of cinnamon at times or lemon rind at others, butter or lard, the bitter salty taste of bicarbonate or the pungent taste of yeast. I blend or mix, integrating other essential ingredients, kneading or whipping until the sadness and yearning in it blends completely with the rest. But no matter what I add, how I make it beautiful and nutritious or decadently rich, if I smooth out its texture or not, the basic ingredients—the facts—remain the same:

By a lake in a foreign land, I glimpsed the man destined for me. I obeyed the dictates of my intuition and my instinct for survival. I also considered the impact my actions would have on my son's life, thus mine. I asked for time to make a decision that could obviously not be postponed. Of my own free will to a large extent, I walked away from the life I was destined to have lived. And I rewrote my own life story.

NORTH AND WEST OF MEMORY: CINE NIGHTS

THE POINSETTIAS WERE ALREADY IN FULL BLOOM. Orion had jockeyed into a position of prominence amid the constellations in the late autumn sky when December arrived. The soft wind underscored the story of a yet unborn baby boy, come to all of us as the savior of humanity, but whose life was fated to end thirty-three years later on a cross.

December came with piñatas filled with peanuts and candy for the children, and days of religious fervor and nights of revelry for the adults. It also came with bags of unfulfilled dreams and promises of finally making them a reality in the next twelve months. New Year's Eve came all too soon for everyone in Jáltipan, but I, for one, was glad. Cine nights would resume in January.

The Cine Anona, our makeshift movie house, was given that name because there was a *palo de anona*—a sugar-apple tree—in its yard. The Anona was really a large empty hall next to a warehouse used by the Sotavento Region Truck Drivers Union for their meetings and parties. A peso for adults and a twenty-cent piece for children would get us all in.

Early on movie nights, as if in processions to a shrine, people from all parts of town arrived at the Cine Anona. They carried their own seats or stools, and cushions and pillows for the children to sit on, to enjoy the latest Superman or Tarzan adventure, or the comic misadventures of Cantinflas, a beloved Mexican comedian, among many other films. All American movies were dubbed into Spanish and had the stamp of approval from the parish. Without the priest's blessing, no movie would be shown in town.

Many of the ladies also carried plenty of Mexican lace-bordered hankies when the newest Mexican tearjerker was shown. We children sniffled or giggled at the emotional or hilarious scenes, but mostly empathized with the adult chorus of sobs or lilting laughter.

"Why are they all crying, then laughing?" I once asked Víctor.

"I don't know. Just do the same or they might never bring us to the movies again," he replied.

I followed his lead. Cine nights were my all-time favorite.

The audience expressed without hesitation their approval or disapproval of the characters' behavior on the screen or the way they handled this or that problem. They often talked to the characters on the screen as if they were three-dimensional and performing right before them on stage.

The men warned a hero about the villain waiting in ambush.

"He's right behind you. Watch out!"

"Hit him! What are you waiting for?"

In a romantic triangle, the young ingénue seemed fascinated by the suave, handsome but not-so-honest man, while the decent, hardworking, generous, loving man went unnoticed. Instead of talking to her aloud, the younger women among us sighed often and whispered in one another's ears.

The older women tried to give advice to the young woman on the screen, warning her that she was infatuated with the wrong man, that her heart really belonged to the other, the good man.

"How can this be? Please. C'mon, girl."

"For God's sake, you're such a fool."

"You prefer that ruffian over the man who's good to you. It's going to cost you. You're going to pay for it. You'll see!"

But when the triangle involved two women—the ingénue and the vixen—and the good guy was about to make the "wrong" choice, they would sigh and say, "The fox, that floosie, she has him under her spell."

At the end of the movie, everyone applauded when good triumphed over evil, redemption came to those in need of it, or when in the end true love, not bewitching passion, won out.

The chair-carrying pilgrims walked their paths back to their homes after the show was over, and people talked animatedly, approving or voicing their disgust at what they had seen or heard. Some of the older men and women complained if any of the actors or actresses stepped out of their hero/heroine characters and played roles of people with even a tiny mar on a sterling reputation. Everything ended well if they of their own volition sacrificed their lives or a rosy future for the greater good.

We children pretended to be the heroes or the damsels in distress in the jungle or Metropolis, pledging to get together the next day and have a contest to see who could swing best on vines from tree to tree or to brick fences. We were ready to re-enact Tarzan's or Superman's supreme feats as they fought villains and saved innocent people or wild animals from death or prison. Mothers, including mine, trembled when they heard us talking and made sure they had plenty of medication, home remedies and other supplies for the next two weeks to take care of our bruises and cuts, twisted or sprained joints.

More modern movie houses in the larger towns around Jálti-pan had bigger real screens and newer projectors that didn't break down or tear the film as often. No one had to carry their seats with them, since the movie theater provided them.

At times, I was asked to act as a chaperone to my older female cousins when they started dating, and their beaus would take them to the cinema in another town. I loved play-ing that role. In an effort to impress my cousins, their boyfriends would buy me chocolate candy to have during the show. They also wanted to keep me busy and content, so I would not notice their fingers caressing my cousins' arms, run-ning softly up their cheeks and across the nape and a shoulder, or their lips coming close but never touching. Although noth-ing went unnoticed by me, I wasn't about to give up a good thing. So I shamelessly lied every time I was asked if any hanky-panky had gone on between the love birds.

At the Cine Anona, however, even in the dark, holding hands, let alone sneaking a kiss, was only possible for the movie stars on the screen. We were all held in a trance-like state by those projected images on a white cloth nailed to the wall. We marveled at the power of a gesture or a look that could express the unmitigated grief for a good husband taken in the prime of his life or a child fallen victim to a disease or an accident. Gestures conveyed the breathtaking anguish of forbidden passion or unrequited love. The ineffable opales-cence of love or the fiery flame of desire reflected on the sur-face of eyes that told a story of ill-fated lovers without a word ever spoken. We felt for those who eked out a living or were hardly rewarded by life in any way. Those who remained solid and stoically good, honest people, who found joy in small things and simple pleasures every day and comfort in one another.

We were already living in San Luis Potosí when we heard that the truckers' union hall had accidentally burned to the ground during a cine night. There were only minor injuries among the moviegoers. As it was our family annual tradition, we spent the next December in Jáltipan. My dad blew air through his mouth as he and I inspected the damage to the old Cine Anona.

"Something better will come of it. It's the way of progress. They'll be building a new, real movie house soon," he told me.

I shared his confidence. For a town so passionate about movies that they would carry their seats to and from the union hall, there was no choice. A new theater was built on the out-skirts of town, with comfortable seats, a more modern projec-tor and a larger screen mounted on the wall. People still walked to the new movie house, but no one was ever again seen carrying their seats or stools, pillows or cushions through town to watch the show.

I was pleased that in San Luis there were five movie hous-es. Twice a month, until we were in our early teens, my broth-er Víctor, my sister Conchita and I went to the Saturday mati-nee at one of three movie houses that showed age-appropriate films for us. We often got home to find my parents getting ready to go to the movies, as was their custom every Saturday evening. I, as the oldest daughter, was left in charge of my younger siblings.

Higher income families in San Luis owned television sets, stereo consoles, stacks and stacks of records, and many other appliances and machines. At home, we didn't have a TV until our parents could afford one, when I was fourteen. Prior to that, my siblings and I would stop and watch through the win-dows of stores that sold TV sets. Any moving image on a screen immediately caught our attention, but not having a TV at home didn't make a difference to us in general. After doing our homework, we would get together and play with our friends in the neighborhood, listen to the radio or talk on the phone. With my mom's help, my sister and I would design and make our dresses based on the styles we would see young women wearing on the TVs in the stores.

When we finally got a TV set, my younger brothers were allowed to watch a half hour of cartoons just before supper and an hour on Saturday mornings. My sister and I watched early-evening Mexican comedies twice a week. All of us watched American weekly series, including "*La ley del revolver*—Gunsmoke" and later "Perry Mason." I couldn't have enough of Perry's eyes. From time to time, I also wondered what he sounded like in gringo English.

My mom watched one *telenovela* in the late afternoon, just before we got home from school. At the time, Mexican soap operas were scripted for TV from published novels, serialized in one-hour daily episodes and sprinkled with commercials throughout. My father never missed late Saturday-night boxing, especially when Casius Clay-Mohammed Ali was slated to fight. My dad considered Clay/Ali an artist of pugilism and early on predicted the boxer would become a legendary heavyweight champion. Ali was definitely the most fun to watch, as he walked into the arena wearing a fighter's mini-robe, not considered proper ring attire for fighters at the time. He then pranced and danced around his opponents, taunting them until he was ready to let them have it. It didn't always work out for Ali, but that didn't matter much to my dad. He was the boxer's fan for life.

Despite all the fun we had when we watched our favorite TV programs, nothing compared to the experience of going to a movie theater to see a film. The large screen made even the smallest of lives seem important. The aroma of vanilla ice cream and popcorn made younger people feel the taste of luxury. Older folks looked forward to the happy ending, which would help them transcend their troubles, if only for 90 minutes at a time. In movie-lovers' minds, going to the movies was as communal an experience as a social celebration with friends and family after Catholic sacramental rites, such as a baptism, a first communion or a wedding.

At age sixteen, after graduating from high school and about to start my first year of dentistry school, I had earned the right to go to the cinema on Sunday afternoons with girlfriends and boyfriends. When the feature showing was considered appropriate for her age, my sister Conchita became my chaperone. My boyfriends liked my sister's lightheartedness and her sense of humor very much. Although they regaled her with popcorn, soda and candy, the goodies were considered a gift not a bribe for her silence. In the tradition of the chaperones in our family, however, my sister made sure that my parents had nothing to worry about.

The theaters in San Luis ranged from modestly furnished with cheaper prices for lower income people to the more expensively furnished theaters with lush velvet drapes flanking balcony sections and frescoes and relief work on the walls. However, all the theaters also had seating to accommodate everyone's financial situation.

One of the cinemas showed only Mexican films, some of them highly censored by the Catholic Church. Some of these films had scantily dressed women or were set in cabaret-type establishments, with sensual Tongolele-like dancers or singers such as the voluptuous, shapely, tightly clad torch singer María Victoria. Some others featured the Pachuco comic Tin-Tan from the Tepito barrio in Mexico City. The rest of the restricted movies were about murder or mayhem in the underbelly of the capital, where supposedly all the criminals lived. Anyone who dared see these movies was advised to go to confession right after leaving the theater, before *la muerte* found them and *el diablo* took them straight to Hell.

Another movie house showed foreign films. Once, when I had just turned seventeen and was in my first year of dentistry school, I went with two of my male classmates to see a church-censored Brigitte Bardot film. Regardless of the content or questionable scenes in any of them, all of Bardot's movies were rated inappropriate for anyone "decent."

Both my classmates were the oldest in our class. I was the youngest. JJ and his brother owned a small clothing store in a neighboring town. He spent his weekends and vacations tending his store there, so he could have the funds to pay tuition and other school expenses. He was a church-going, weekly confession Catholic. Handsome XC was also a Catholic, but his father and grandparents were from Spain. They were as reverent toward Catholicism as they were critical of the Church and the government. He loved acting and every so often had minor roles in small revue companies. He had a beautiful voice and could be heard sometimes reciting poetry on the radio.

We had been studying hard for a midterm and were already convinced that we would ace the exam. So XC convinced both of us to go with him to see the Bardot movie. So I wouldn't be recognized, I wore a kerchief around my head and sunglasses. He bought the tickets, then the three of us walked in. No one stopped me.

JJ spent most of the time with his right hand over his face, but sneaked looks at the sexy Bardot through the slits between his index and middle fingers. There were hardly any nude scenes but lots of comic ones. The movie was subtitled, so JJ was also missing what was said. XC slapped JJ's hand a few times, asking, "Why did you come to see this movie? C'mon, man, it's only a comedy." I had as much fun watching the interaction between my classmates as watching Bardot's funny mishaps in the movie.

After the movie, JJ rushed to the cathedral a block away to find a priest and confess his sins, which I was sure were all "sins of the mind." XC walked me to the bus stop. He didn't seem eager to talk. I made some comments about the differences between Italian, American and French comedies, and talked about my preference for Italian comedies. When I was ready to board the bus, he said, "You're one of the smartest and prettiest girls I know. Don't let anything or anyone change you." It was one of the best compliments I ever got, and I owed it all to Brigitte Bardot! Our friendship ended when I started going steady with Guillermo Hernández, whom he believed wasn't the man for me. Two years later, he was invited to our wedding, but he was the only one of my classmates who didn't show up.

When my husband Guillermo and I arrived in Berkeley in 1964, I was happy to see many movie theaters that showed not only American but also foreign films, and some also had classic movie revivals. Guillermo and I would save every penny possible to go to a matinee every other Sunday, as we had done in San Luis during our courtship. My comprehension and reading skills in English were not that great at the time, and subtitled foreign films were difficult for me to follow. So Guillermo chose those films he felt would not be too boring or too hard for me. In the theater, I sat there in the dark, holding my husband's hand and warning him not to translate for me what was being said. I used my imagination to guess what the story was about. I paid close attention to the looks and gestures, the happy, mischievous or crooked smile, a frown, the spark in an eye, the tear or the gasp held back, the intended gentleness or aggression of a raised hand. This was the silent language that had guided me since my Cine Anona days to get to the heart and soul of the story. At home, I would recount my version of the story to him, and we would laugh at my misunderstanding and confusion. Yet I was right in my perceptions and understanding of the story at least half of the time. He would take me to see old films that I or the two of us had already seen in San Luis. From time to time, we went to see a film by the Spanish director Luis Buñuel or some other Latin American filmmaker.

When we saw a revival of *To Kill a Mockingbird*, I was absolutely fascinated to hear Gregory Peck speak in his native language, not sounding at all like his dubbed voice in Spanish. Voice in its original language became a matter of paramount importance for me. It wasn't just the way a word sounded in English. Each word I was learning carried the weight of the culture that had given birth to it, that had molded and shaped it and given it meaning. I hadn't given much consideration to this notion of voice since my third year of elementary school in Jáltipan, when I used to stand on a stepping stool and recite patriotic poems in public.

Silent or spoken language gave voice to a culture. Voice and culture comprised a single, living organism that never stopped mutating because the people in whom it lived continued to adapt to, accept or reject new customs, conditions or new ideas. I realized then that I would never speak English well enough unless I familiarized myself with the culture that made it what it was, that provided me with the social context, and that made words and concepts powerful. To gain access to it, I had to speak with *norteamericanos*—Anglo Americans—as often as possible. I was a fast learner, and I was attending the English for Foreign-Born program at the old McKinley Continuation High School on Dwight Way in Berkeley five hours a day.

I decided that it was best to have short periods of conversation with the regulars, who rode the bus every day at the same time I did. The men sat or stood hanging onto a strap, reading newspaper sections folded in four. Those sitting usually got up when any woman got on and ceded the seat to her. I quickly realized that the men on the bus would not be very open to have a conversation with a young woman who spoke half-chewed English. Whenever they did, they couldn't help themselves and immediately set out to play the role of Professor Higgins to a very reluctant Eliza Doolittle.

I chose to sit next to older ladies, who even in the mid-1960s still wore hats and gloves when out and about town. They were always thrilled that a young woman, perhaps the same age as a daughter or granddaughter at home, would enjoy talking with them. The English lesson from the ladies came just before my stop when they would suggest I use a different expression than the one I had incorrectly used. From one of them, I also learned my first idiomatic expression, "That's the way the cookie crumbles," which I understood as the equivalent of "*Así pasa. Pues, ni modo*," in Spanish.

To aid in my language-learning goals, Guillermo's sister, Frieda, and her husband, Bob, came to visit us and brought us the gift of a small portable TV, suggesting that I watch it for at least a couple of hours daily. I resisted the idea. First, I was not used to watching TV. Second, some programs, such as newscasts and comedies, required cultural understanding and comprehension skills beyond my grasp at the time. Guillermo, who spoke English well, insisted on my taking the TV set from room to room as I did my housework or cooked dinner. It took every bit of discipline I had in me to watch such soap operas as "General Hospital" and "The Newlyweds," and such reruns of programs as "Leave it to Beaver," "Voyage to the Bottom of the Sea" and "McHale's Navy." Listening to McHale, played by Ernest Borgnine, I learned my second idiom, "Knock it off, (you guys)," an expression that has come in handy many times in my life.

TV viewing was a good way to learn English and become acquainted with some aspects of the culture. My vocabulary definitely expanded. Watching commercials was more helpful than regular programming. A capitalist mind someplace in the western world came up with the "brilliant" idea of not only showing the image of a product, but using spoken and written descriptions. Glamorous, well-groomed males or females of various ages illustrated its uses. Finally, a catchy jingle would help the consumer remember the product advertised. By watching TV ads, I was able to practice all four language skills many times in capsules of ten seconds or less.

Cultural elements were present in films as they were also in television programs. No doubt TV ads reflected the role consumerism played in American society. I never made the mistake of thinking that Hollywood films or TV programs represented U.S. culture, or the California brand of it, in its entirety. I knew that if I really wanted to find out what people's values, myths, beliefs, lore and other aspects unique to the culture were about, I had to read not only newspapers or trendy magazines but the literature produced at the time. So I decided to read the books on which the movie scripts were based to get to a competitive proficiency level. Then I could try reading other works.

I started with Harper Lee's novel *To Kill a Mockingbird* because I had already seen the film twice and knew the stories in it well. I found it inspiring. In addition, I was also partial to it because the children in it reminded me of Víctor and me, and *el loco* Andrés, in Jáltipan, but reading it wasn't as easy as I thought at first. Nonetheless, armed with a Webster in one hand and a Larousse Spanish-English dictionary in the other, I read the novel in English. For the first time, the differences between the writing of a book and the scripting of a film became clearer and provided me with insights as to both genres, and the interdependence between writing and moviemaking.

As a writer, I have benefited from watching films as much as reading the books they're based on. I do know that the success or failure of a book or a movie depends on the ability—the art—of the writer or the filmmaker to tell a good story.

I was recently reminded of this interdependence between moviemaking and literature while sitting at a theater watching *Avatar*. There is no question that this film's extraordinary special effects and the mind-boggling possibilities for bio-sciences offered by technology in it are well rendered. I only wish that Jim Cameron had given the story in it more attention. It is at best mediocre. But I'm glad I went to see it, because it reaffirmed my belief that good storytelling in films as in literature still matters. I can only hope that the symbiotic relationship between literature and filmmaking is not a thing of the past.

Movies and books, as well as music and poetry, are the sensory and sensual concoctions I consume often to sustain my spirit during unhealthy and insane times in the history of this our modern world. With the exception of some films where it is obvious that either the director or the actors have little respect for their art, and for my intelligence as a movie lover, I have seen A, B or C movies and have always found something to praise in them. If shown on TV, like a child, I can watch all-time favorites and still be delighted by the antics, adventure, intrigue and romance or thrilled by the murder and mayhem in them time and again.

In sixty years, I have been to many movie theaters, large or small, modest or posh, with soft rocking seats or plain wooden chairs, carpet or linoleum flooring, showing old, black-and-

white or color movies on narrow or on wide screens with sur-
round sound. I have watched movies sitting on the floor of my
living room, with friends or alone. I have never lost my desire
for "going to the movies" and sharing the experience with relatives, friends or perfect strangers on all sides. There in the
dark we are all transfixed by the power of the story and of
actors that will remain alive long after their stars have expired.
They remain as real in my subconscious mind as the Cine
Anona: The place where the story reigned supreme, where all
fantasies and dreams were possible if only one was willing to
drag a chair through town to a makeshift movie house and
back home again at the end of cine nights.

ALSO KNOWN AS: *A WOMAN'S NAMES*

AS IT WAS THE TRADITION IN MEXICO, forty days after I saw the light for the first time, my birth was registered at the Office of Vital Statistics in Jáltipan de Morelos, Veracruz. As expected, both my parents were present in the office to attest to my true paternal and maternal bloodlines and to claim for me the rights to which I was entitled under the law. They and their representatives, my godparents, were all present at the church when I was baptized. On my behalf, they took the oath to make sure that I would uphold the tenets of the Catholic faith and renounce evil. I was registered and baptized with the given name Luz del Carmen.

In the Christian tradition, children were usually given biblical names: Isaac, Aaron, Abraham, Joseph, Solomon, David et al for boys; Miriam (María) Ruth, Esther, Eva, Sarah, among others, were appropriate for girls. In the New Testament, the names of the apostles and the women who accompanied Christ in his journey up to Mount Calvary had also been very popular in other Christian religions.

In the Catholic tradition, parents were able to check the calendar of saints and find the names of those saints in charge on their child's day of birth. There were more saints than days in the year. Sometimes parents were faced with as many as ten names per day, not counting the many names the Virgin Mary was known by. Thus, they chose to name their baby after one or more of their patron saints. Together with guardian angels, these saintly souls looked after the children on earth or interceded on their behalf in the celestial courts.

A hierarchy existed everywhere; Heaven and Hell were not excluded from establishing a pecking order. Some parents wanted their children's advocates in heaven as on earth to be the most powerful or erudite. Topping most parents' lists, were the names of saints who had been kings, who had also done a lot of good for their own people and had spread the word of Christ throughout their kingdoms. In second place were the names of the princes or great theologians of the faith, and those who suffered torture and torment rather than betraying the purity of their souls: Luis/Luisa, Enrique/Enriqueta, Guillermo/Guillermina, Agustín/Agustina, Tomás/Tomasa, Pablo/Paula, Pedro/Petra, Sebastián/Sebastiana, among many others.

Regardless of the saint's gender or celestial status, if a girl was born on April 13, she would be named Hermenegilda or Quintiliana, according to the calendar of saints. The masculine names would of course be spelled the same except for an "o" replacing the feminine "a." Not in a million years would my parents have agreed to give me any of the above names! And, of course, when I was a teenager I thanked them.

My mother was a poet, unpublished because she never wanted to submit her work for publication. She wrote lines or entire poems on any paper at hand, such as pieces of newspapers ads, blood-stained butcher paper, gift wrap, paper sacks, pages torn from our old school notebooks or her log of daily expenses. She wrote while she cooked or did her housework. From time to time, my father went through the house, gathering her poems; he typed and saved them for her and us. But by the time my father found them, my mother had already memorized her poems and was able to recite them at will. Perhaps the sensitivity and sensibility of the poet in my mom moved her to exert serious deliberation in naming her children. By the time each of us was born, the most auspicious and melodic combinations of appellatives awaited us. My father always approved of her choices.

My names automatically put me under the protection of Our Lady of Light (Luz) and Our Lady of the Mount Carmel— (Carmen, in its Spanish spelling). In my case, she had also selected those names for me for their personal meaning to her, which the poet in her interpreted as "*luminaria encantadora*— charming or spellbinding light or luminescence." Obviously, *luz* means light, no matter the context or the function it's attached to, and the term is used in general to denote its essence, brightness or other qualities. For example, in Mexico and other Latin American countries, to give birth to a baby is equivalent to bringing her or him to light or to enlightenment—*dar a luz*.

I had no difficulty making my mom's etymological connection with my first given name. However, Carmen was a different story. Sure that my mother had made up the origin and meaning of Carmen, or stretched the truth to suit her purpose, as she was known to do from time to time, I once looked for the meaning of my second name. My first encounter was with the young gypsy Carmen in Bizet's opera. Although I was passionate about many things in life, I didn't see much similarity between the operatic Carmen and myself. Apparently, in Granada, Spain, the word Carmen meant orchard or garden. There were plenty of orchards and vineyards on Mount Carmel, which had prompted some Catholic faithful to affirm that Carmen meant "the Lord's vineyard." Somewhere else it was also used to designate a type of poetic composition. But I never found any correlation between Carmen and my mom's intended significance for this name as "enchanting or bewitching."

As a teenager, I asked my father about the significance of a name. Why did he and especially my mother give great importance to our names? My father chuckled and reminded me about a comical scene in the movie *El Padrecito—The Young Priest*, in which Cantinflas plays the role of a newly ordained priest sent to a rural church to help the ailing, older parish priest, who is about to retire. Among other duties, El Padrecito is expected to impart all of the Sacraments, beginning with Baptism. When a couple brings their baby boy to the baptismal font and want to name him Nepomuceno, El Padrecito refuses to give the baby that name. He explains that their innocent baby will have to bear that name for the rest of his life, and it isn't fair. Thus, he sends them home and asks that they come back with a more likeable name.

My father added his own pinch-of-salt wisdom to the baptismal name story: "Even if a child's life turns out to be ordinary or the child is ordinary looking, everyone deserves to have a great or beautiful name, a name someone can be proud of, that people will always remember and enjoy saying."

I loved my given name, which I heard only when my parents introduced me to friends or acquaintances and at home only when my mom was upset with me. If my mother called me by my given name, followed by a "*ven acá—*come here," I immediately knew I was being summoned to account for some wrongdoing. At school, my teachers and classmates also called me Luz del Carmen.

We Mexicans, however, are very fond of using diminutives of names and nicknames, which can be positive or negative. Those nicknames become part of anyone's personal and family history and might even shape their personalities. Take, for example, my maternal grandfather, whose name was Diódoro Constantino. Because he had a short flat nose, a pug-nose, he was known as El Chato in life as in memoriam. A bear of a man but the youngest and only male in the Stevens family, who had a tile, granite and marble workshop and store in San Luis Potosí, was called "El Nene—the baby," by his older sisters, even when his hair had already turned the color of wispy cirrus clouds.

Throughout my life, regardless of where I've lived, I've answered to my nickname Lucha, which means "struggle or fight." As beautiful as my given name is, during my infancy and childhood, I became Luchita to my parents and relatives; my cousin Dulce María still calls me Luchita, even now, at ages seventy-two and sixty-eight, respectively. Luz del Carmen or Lucha/Luchita? As I think most people normally do, I developed a separate public persona that complemented my nickname.

I, as Luz del Carmen, loved school and learning and reflected on concepts and ideas. I thought about justice and destiny from an early age, I could spend a long time by myself, sewing, working on puzzles, listening to music, stories and poetry on the radio, or playing the piano, reading, and later writing stories or poems. As Lucha, I was the social being. I didn't mind participating in public activities such as piano recitals. I competed in spelling bees, even if I made mistakes or didn't win. I also enjoyed dancing, going to the movies, playing ping-pong, chess and poker or canasta with classmates and friends. With my father, I attended a variety of events, including plays and concerts at the theater, and rodeos and bullfights at the arena. Since I was my mother's helper, I also had a handle on the practical things in life, and learned how to sew, cook, bake, clean house, wash laundry by hand and take care of my younger siblings.

Like everyone else's full name throughout Mexico, mine included my first and middle names, followed first by my father's last name then my mother's family name. My mother's surname would be dropped once I got married and I became a member of my husband's family. Reluctantly or willingly I would then take his family name as mine, preceded by the possessive "*de*—of." When I got married and after three weeks moved to Berkeley, all of that changed. My struggle to keep my full name and a nickname and my two personas intact began.

From August 29, 1964 on, my mother's family name disappeared from any and all of my legal documents, including my green card. Hernández, my husband's surname, was added to my name after the possessive *de*. I was given no choice by both my own family and my in-laws, or the rest of society, south or north of the border for that matter. This was the socially and legally acceptable way. Although for a long time I thought that the use of *de* was popular all over Latin America and Spain, I found out that in Chile, Uruguay, Argentina, Cuba and Spain, women were able to keep their maiden names regardless of marital status. They included paternal and maternal surnames.

I asked myself why in other Latin American nations, the use of *de* before a husband's surname was socially and legally mandatory. Presumably, the use of the possessive preposition *de* gained popularity during medieval times, when many people in a variety of places in the Asian, African and European continents did not use a family or matrilineal surname yet as a form of identification. Western literature is full of first names followed by *de* and the name of a birthplace or residence town. Servants and slaves used *it* to denote the name of the master or household they served. At times, a son of a man named Martín could use his given name and add *ez* to his father's name, then use it as a surname. I'm not sure when the practice of adding both patrilineal and matrilineal surnames to a name began, but it certainly made long and longer names possible. My names and surnames combined were as long as an eighteen-wheel semi, but I loved them.

In the English for Foreign-Born program I attended in Berkeley, I learned that in English a word that had more than three syllables was considered too long. Monosyllables abounded and long words were shortened to one or two brief syllables and sometimes reduced down to just the initials. Laboratory was lab; medical doctors MD's, high fidelity Hi-Fi, science fiction Sci-Fi and so on. People's names went through this transformation as well. William was Will or Bill; Frederick Fred; Richard Rick or Rich. Constance was Connie, Catherine Cathy, Elizabeth Liz or Beth. It was all right to use a nickname for a U.S. president, or reduce his name but enhance the importance of his legacy by using the capitals: JFK, FDR, for example. Dwight D. Eisenhower was simply Ike. President Clinton was Bill not William.

I found this custom of name/word reductionism intriguing, as I do nowadays seeing the transformation of words like technician into tech, technological into techno or a president into a Prez, let alone uses like Google as a verb. Back in 1964-65, I didn't know English well-enough to ask anyone for clarification. To most monolingual English-speakers, my questions might not have made any sense and they would have probably dismissed my queries as a non-English-speaker's nonsense. By comparison and contrast of uses and practices in daily life, these linguistic idiosyncrasies in any culture become more evident to second-language learners, but the intimate relationship between culture and language is undeniable anywhere in the world.

One day, while waiting for the bus in downtown Berkeley, I finally figured out the reason for the need to reduce words to their minimal abbreviations or forms while leaving the meaning untouched. I was watching socially diverse old, young, middle-aged American individuals come and go, and in the midst of street traffic as they tried to cross streets. People were in too much of a hurry to get someplace, anyplace. I wondered if they all really knew where they were going. Business and busyness were one and the same. I watched as a car driver in a hurry tried to pass and get in front of a bus, which had been slowed by other cars in front of it. Risking being hit by an oncoming car or causing problems for other drivers, the impatient driver had to speed up and quickly maneuver to wedge his vehicle in between the bus and another car, gaining only a car's length advantage.

That day, I realized that people in the United States were constantly on the move, wanting things done yesterday, and were not used to waiting long for results. American English reflected this culture that erred almost always on the entitlements of the individual, on the side of action, even when futile and perilous, and on perpetual motion, especially upward mobility in any and all areas of human endeavor. It was no wonder that this fast-paced aspect of U.S. business culture was called "the rat race." My sister-in-law, Frieda, and her husband, Robert Yeaton, distilled this philosophy, inherited for the most part from the Puritans, to a rhyme easy to understand: "Early to bed, early to rise, work like hell and exercise."

Relaxation and reflection were not given as much importance as in other cultures. Many immigrants such as Latin Americans and particularly Mexicans, and other non-immigrant peoples of color such as Native Americans and Blacks, were in general considered lazy for not adhering to the Puritan philosophy. But public opinion concerning who in reality we the immigrants from any country or culture in the world were was based on assumptions. I have never been part of a group or seen people who have worked hard and harder for what they've needed or wanted than recent immigrants, regardless of their nationality. Unlike citizens, they have no guarantees for survival other than their own work; they don't feel entitled and have only a few protections under the law.

Some of the newly arrived immigrants came with names unheard of before in the United States and felt pressured to change their given names to Anglo-American names. During 1964 and 1965, however, being called by my full name plus my married name—Luz del Carmen Corpi de Hernández—required too great an effort for English-speakers, who got impatient and, feeling embarrassed, ended up joking about the length of my name. Tired of it and to soften the blows to my ego, I decided to shorten my name by using my first name, followed by my paternal last name, then my married last name, Luz Corpi Hernández. Unfortunately I forgot that Corpi would be reduced to the initial C or eliminated altogether.

In fact, I became a totally different entity on paper, not counting the various spellings and pronunciations my name underwent. Read or said aloud by monolingual English-speakers, Luz sounded to me too much like "loss," and unless I spelled Luz out, my name would be written down as Luce. When they did pronounce my maiden surname, people often dropped the "i" in Corpi. There were times my name seemed to mean "the corporation of loss." Nothing was left of the luminescence my mother had intended to be so much a part of it, thus of me.

Frequently, I felt I was living a borrowed existence, life as an alias, with a name that was like an old, broken down truck made up of rusted, recycled parts and pieces, taken from different makes and models. Saying my name and spelling it became a daily chore, everywhere I was, and especially on the phone. As surely as a constant dribble of water eventually erodes a stone, this daily name trauma caused my self-esteem to diminish in worth for a long while.

At home, my husband, like the few new friends we had, called me Lucha (loo-tcha), but the pronunciation of my nickname also became a struggle for other English-speakers, since the "ch" between two vowels is often pronounced as a "k" in English. So I ended up with my nickname pronounced as "Luka." Sigh!!

When I was pregnant, Guillermo and I gave much thought to our baby's name. My husband favored having a girl, but in the end, the sex of the baby mattered little to both of us. Regardless of gender, we would love our baby. Neither of us wanted to give the baby any of our names, or a name already handed down from generation to generation. We considered names of family members on both sides and decided against them. The same happened to Victoria, my mother's name, and Frieda, my mother-in-law's name. At the time, my husband was fascinated by the works and philosophy of Søren Kierkegaard, and of course the Dane philosopher's first name topped my husband's list, followed by Erik. I liked the name Marina Luz but, fearing than Luz would be often mispronounced, I leaned more toward the name Luisa Eugenia for a daughter and Arturo Enrique for a son—Arturo was my youngest brother-in-law's name and Enrique my husband's middle name. We both liked those choices, in case we didn't come up with any other names before our baby was born. At the time of my son's birth, as planned, we registered him as Arturo Enrique. Fortunately, he likes his name and has always insisted on being called Arturo, never Arthur or Art.

In 1970, when I filed for divorce, I considered the potentially negative impact taking my maiden name would have on my very young son. I decided not to take it back so that we would both have the same family name. Later and thanks to the Women's Liberation Movement, we had choices other generations of women before us hadn't, such as keeping our maiden names to begin with, not just taking it back after a divorce. We were no longer required to checkmark the "divorced" or "married" status on most employment, credit or health forms. Instead of Miss or Mrs. we could simply X the Ms. box. But my son was still very young, and my common sense dictated that I wait to change my name, to avert any social difficulties in the school milieu for him.

While I did clerical work at Wells Fargo Bank, at U.C. Berkeley and later as a Cal undergraduate student, all of my official documents bore my former husband's surname. Everyone knew I was his former wife, especially at Chicano Studies, where he was also a teaching assistant. I had been a temporary program assistant at Chicano Studies. Later, I became a MEChA student representative on the Executive Committee. Composed of faculty, students and community organizers, it was the policy-making body for the program.

I turned a deaf ear to all the rumors floating around about my divorce and my husband's very young girlfriend. I wanted Chicanos and Chicanas around me to see me not as Hernández's ex-wife but as the woman and the person I was. Yet, even though I knew these people were not ill-intentioned, their insecurities made them insensitive and sometimes cruel. I ignored them, and only entrusted my innermost thoughts and feelings to three or four good friends. I learned to keep my composure under pressure, live my life by my own beliefs and convictions, and keep both my son's and my life out of public scrutiny as much as possible.

At that time, I had published a couple of poems as Luz C. Hernández, but I felt unhappy about it. My relationship with my former husband had opened up avenues of thought and learning and, while married to him, I had grown intellectually as never before. The few times I talked about him in public, I referred to him as one of the most influential men in my life, next to my father. He deserved the credit and my gratitude, but not for any of my writings, the content in them or for the positive or negative criticism they elicited. Why, how and what I wrote about remained entirely my prerogative and responsibility. As a mother of a very young child, I had no choice, but as a poet I was able to exercise the options open to me. Thus, I decided to combine my nickname and my father's surname and took Lucha Corpi as my pen name.

In 1973, after having completed my coursework at Cal, my son Arturo and I moved to East Oakland. For years, I had been a board member of Aztlán Cultural, an arts service organization in Berkeley. It later merged with Centro Chicano de Escritores—Chicano Writers Center. I was the center's first president. I had also done volunteer work as a dental assistant, three evenings a week, at the Clínica de La Raza (The Fruitvale Health Project). I was also interested in working toward the establishment of pre-school programs in the Oakland Public Schools.

Nancy Reagan, first lady of California at the time, was asked if the state should subsidize childcare centers through California's Department of Education. She publicly maintained that a woman's—a mother's—place was at home with the children. With one statement, she wiped out the possibility for thousands of single mothers in California. Many of them were women of color who needed help with reliable childcare to finish school or to obtain gainful employment. The only choice left for us was to become welfare recipients or work much harder to support ourselves and our children. Although it was too late for me and other women, who were paying one-third of our salaries in childcare, I joined the Comité Popular Educativo de La Raza—La Raza for People's

Education Committee—a grassroots Oakland organization. Made up of teachers, parents and other community members, its goal was to exert pressure at the local and state levels to develop viable bilingual education programs in elementary schools, children's centers and adult education.

The work we were doing at the time brought us together as a group and helped to cement our mutual respect and love for one another. Many friendships were formed and grew stronger then and there, in the trenches. We banded together to put pressure on the Oakland Board of Education and the school superintendent Marcus Foster to start a bilingual (Spanish-English) childcare center and elementary school as part of the Oakland Public Schools. From time to time, we also joined forces with Asian (mostly Chinese) and African American organizations in Oakland that were working toward similar goals.

From the very beginning, I found Oakland a fascinating city. There were at least 80 major languages spoken daily. Its population was comprised of African Americans, Anglo Americans, Latinos and many people from all over the world, who co-existed, or tried to, in integrated neighborhoods and schools. Oakland was my kind of urban community: a truly multilingual, multicultural city, where the American Dream was dreamt in many languages and reflected many cultures, some of which had been unknown to me until then. For these parents, as for me, the road to the fulfillment of a dream began with their children's education.

When El Centro Infantil, the first bilingual childcare center for Spanish-speaking pre-schoolers, opened in the early 1970s, its objective wasn't only to provide pre-school instruction and care to the tots, but also to consider that children were members of a family unit. That unit was disrupted if the parents and other adults in it weren't able to function in the larger community. So, one of the center's objectives was also to enable the rest of the family to function in the United States by giving them the linguistic and cultural tools—the life skills—they needed to survive. A new class in survival English and life-skills was being set up for the parents and tailored to their needs. Prospective students were polled and their needs ranged from learning to follow directions on clothes patterns and to convert measurements from metric to inches, feet and yards, and to buying a sewing machine on credit. Opening a bank account, applying for a job, filling out health questionnaires, making appointments or being able to communicate basic needs in English topped the list.

I was hired to teach the class. I had been in the United States almost ten years, five of those years as a single mother, with a school-age child at home. As an immigrant, necessity had been my best teacher, and I had learned to solve the same kinds of problems that my students were facing. I had a B.A. and other minimum requirements for any teacher to obtain a credential, and I applied for an Adult Education Designated Subjects temporary Credential, which had to be renewed after completing a number of units on Adult Education principles, methodology and classroom practicum. Being a teacher had never been my goal. Even though it was part-time, the job paid much more than I had earned as a secretary, especially after I had become a student, and I had to pay back my student loans.

Two months after I started teaching, one Monday morning I walked into my classroom and realized that for the next three hours whatever personal problems I had outside of that room would be relegated to a corner of my mind, to be faced again when I stepped out of my classroom four hours later. Also, the satisfaction of having accomplished something good that day was as priceless as the feeling I experienced every night after my writing sessions. I marveled at life's ironies, for throughout my life in Mexico and the United States, I had never considered pursuing a career as a teacher or writing, and yet, I had been meant to be both an educator and a poet.

Aware of all the trouble Americans had when they tried to pronounce my names, one of my first lessons as an Adult Education teacher to Mexican and Latin American students was on names, pointing out to them that when asked about their last name, they should make sure it was their father's or husband's last name they wrote or said at the end. I also explained to the women who had names like María Elena, María Teresa, María Guadalupe that unless they combined their first and middle names, they would be called only María. The other possibility was to combine both names into one, but that would also make some names long, and they might be faced with ridicule. Some of them decided to drop the María and use only their middle names. The four male students in the class resented having to drop their middle names or reduce them to an initial and also eliminate their maternal surnames. The youngest of them, who had just turned eighteen, loved the idea of using his initials, like J.A. for José Antonio, for example. I advised that they use and spell out their full names on any health, employment or credit forms.

In terms of their children's names, the younger Latina mothers decided to give their baby daughters single names that could be easily pronounced like Lisa, Estefanía, Christina or Adriana, for example. This was already a custom adopted by Chinese parents, who gave their sons and daughters short, easy American first names. Contrary to tradition in China and Taiwan, and in line with usage in the United States, their paternal surnames followed their first names not preceded them.

Other names were chosen by Mexican and Chicana mothers because of their popularity on American TV programs or

Latin American TV soap operas. Names like Yesenia and Yadira popped up for awhile. The calendar of saints as a source of names for the neonates was replaced to a certain extent by the calendar of soap opera characters.

Richard (Ricardo) Rodríguez, a friend of my former husband and of my very good friend Berta Ramona Thayer, had once told me something very interesting when he found out that I watched the primetime soap *Dynasty*. He chuckled and categorically stated, "Chicanas are going to be naming their kids after those characters in *Dynasty*. You'll see."

A couple of months later, I was invited to do a program in San Antonio, Texas. As I walked into a food mart to get some fruit and other munchies to keep in my hotel room, I heard a mother calling her daughter to her by a name that sounded very much like the word "crystal." I was curious when her pretty, bright-eyed three-year-old daughter came running. She had an infectious laughter, so I thought the name fit her well.

"Your daughter has a beautiful name. Do you spell it like 'cristal' in Spanish?" I asked the young mother.

Flattered, she spelled it for me: k-r-y-s-t-l-e. It was the name of the millionaire's second wife in *Dynasty*. I told her I also watched the primetime soap opera, and asked her why she hadn't named her daughter after the man's first wife, Alexis, who also had a beautiful name. "Because that Alexis is the mean one, the witch." We talked for a few minutes longer as she and her daughter were also walking in the direction of my hotel.

As soon as I got back to Oakland, I called Richard and told him the story. He laughed. I also remembered what my dad had said about the importance of a name and how great names shaped the way we were perceived and accepted by others. I felt pleased that my son was happy with his name.

Arturo was around eleven years old when I finally told him I wanted to take back my Corpi last name, but I didn't want to make things difficult for him at school. "It's okay. Go ahead and change your name. I know you're my mom. You'll always be my mom," he replied.

Since Arturo was young, he had spent every summer with both his dad's and my family, mostly in San Luis Potosí and Saltillo, and a couple of times in Jáltipan. I was already saving up money to send him to my sister's in Saltillo so he could attend school there for a year, right after he finished elementary school. This would give him a much longer period of time than just a summer to experience daily and family living in the sociocultural environment that had formed his dad, but to a much larger extent me. It would also help him acquire a larger vocabulary and improve his reading and writing skills in Spanish. Having been born in Berkeley automatically made him a U.S. citizen. Back then, Mexico allowed only the children of two Mexican nationals living abroad to retain the right to their Mexican citizenship. When they reached the age for military service, they had to choose one or the other country. I wanted to keep this option open for my son, although it was becoming clearer to me that Arturo was leaning toward choosing his U.S. citizenship.

At that time, I felt free to seriously consider becoming a naturalized citizen and putting to rest the whole matter of my name. At the swearing-in ceremony, I could choose to keep my name or change it. I told Arturo about my plans. However, he didn't respond as favorably as I thought he would.

"You're not American! You are Mexican, Mom. Mexican!" he stressed, obviously upset.

We had a long talk about it, Although he could not verbalize his feelings entirely, I gathered that he was afraid that I would cut ties with Mexico. As long as I was a Mexican citizen, he would have access to both his extended families and to everything Mexican. I was his vital connection to that part of his own life and his Mexican cultural heritage. I tried to explain that nothing would change in terms of our lives. We would continue spending time with both families in Mexico. But it seemed terribly important to him that I remain a Mexican citizen, and I promised that I wouldn't go ahead with my plans before checking with him again in a few years.

The grueling process of recovering my maiden name ensued. I changed my records at the Social Security Administration first. Immediately after, I got a new driver's license. I applied for a replacement green card bearing the name changes at the Immigration and Naturalization Office, then a revised and protocolized passport and consular ID card at the Mexican Consulate in San Francisco. By the time I had finally changed my employment records, bank and credit accounts, two years had elapsed. If not Luz del Carmen, I was at least Luz Corpi, but I continued publishing under the name of Lucha Corpi.

I would remember this long and arduous process when I wrote *Black Widow's Wardrobe*, a murder mystery about Licia Lecuona, who kills her abusive husband and is sentenced to eighteen years in prison. Upon her release, she's attacked by an unknown assailant, and Chicana detective Gloria Damasco is hired to keep her alive at any cost. Licia asks Gloria whether or not Damasco is her husband's name. Gloria says it is and explains that her husband is dead. She also knows that Lecuona is actually Licia's married name. So Licia, the black widow, replies: "It's hard for a woman to get rid of a husband's name (. . .) Even after she kills him." I was happy I had finally recovered my maiden name, without having to kill a husband.

About that time, a young, attractive Eritrean widow with a young son had joined my morning intermediate ESL class. She had recently been given her refugee status papers. She had to work one day at the Parent Participation class at school so her son could be in the day-care program, and she could attend the ESL classes the rest of the time. She was smart and had had an elementary education in her country. Soon, she was making great progress. Sometimes, she would stay and have her lunch in the room, then help me put things away and get the room ready for my afternoon class. When we talked, she would always refer to herself by a name she liked, not her name on my class roster. "I, Sarah Berhane," she'd say.

Among other things, she told me her husband had been killed during an armed conflict in her country. She and her son had escaped and gone to a refugee camp. Finally, they had arrived in the United States. She was living in her brother-in-law's house, but he and his wife were keeping her food stamps, and he demanded that she turn over most of her Welfare money to him. She was saving as much as she could because she wanted to move out. She needed to get a job, so she and her son would not be sent to another country when her refugee permit expired.

One day, a man came to my classroom door, asking for her. She wasn't in class that day. He seemed very upset when he couldn't find her. I asked him if there was a problem. He said there wasn't and left. It didn't take me long to figure out he was her brother-in-law. The next day, she called me at school to let me know that she and her son were moving out of her brother-in-law's home and into a friend's house. She needed two weeks, then she would be back to school.

She came back to school but only to tell me good-bye because she and her son were moving to Los Angeles. She had a cousin there and she would live with him and his family until she found a job. She was crying and I was trying very hard not to, so I had a hard time putting together what she told me next. Her brother-in-law wanted her to be his second wife and live in the same house with his other family. Apparently, in their country, he had the right to make her his second wife because she was his youngest brother's widow. To protect her and her son, he also wanted and felt entitled to all the marital privileges a husband had. She wanted nothing to do with him. She was free. She lived in America now. But he would never leave her alone. So she was going away. I felt so sad to see her go and I cried with her. We hugged and she left. I probably would not see her again, but she would be better off far away from him.

Obsessed with her, every day for three weeks, he came looking for her. Time and again he asked if she had called, if I had a phone for her. My reply was always the same: She hadn't and I didn't. He finally stopped coming.

A year later, I had to take a day off to go with Arturo to the Mexican consulate to get his visa so he could spend the next school year in Saltillo. The whole subject of my name change came up. We had to wait for a couple of hours for them to track my file number and make sure everything was in order. So I would have to go back to the consulate to pick up the papers in a couple of weeks.

The next day, I walked into my classroom and my lovely Eritrean student was there, all smiles. She had just come back to Oakland. She had a job in a restaurant downtown. I asked her about her situation with her brother-in-law. She said he didn't know she was back. No one had seen him for a long time. Two weeks later, I read in the *Oakland Tribune* that my student had been shot while waiting for a bus in downtown Oakland. The man who killed her didn't flee the scene and had surrendered to the police right away. She had been shot by that man in front of many witnesses, but for as yet unknown reasons. The killer's and his victim's names were given. It was my student's name. I was in shock and my heart immediately went to her young son, now an orphan. The paper also gave the killer's name, but I had never known her brother-in-law's name. It had to be, but obviously his name was very different from hers. I wasn't surprised because I knew that a woman in her country didn't have to take her husband's family name. Later, I learned her brother-in-law was the man who had shot her. Her cousin in L.A. had come to take her little boy to live with him and his family. I found comfort in that.

For me, she would always be "I, Sarah Berhane," the name she had liked for herself. What good would it have done that she had the name she liked? What magic was there in a name that could ensure a woman's survival and protect her from violence anywhere in the world?

When school was out for me, I took my son to Saltillo. He would spend the year going to school there and living with my sister Conchita and her family. There he fit in nicely between his two male cousins, with whom he had spent part of his summers. Guillermo also had three other sons. For the first time, Arturo also had two "sisters," my nieces, and he had to learn to relate to them.

When he returned to California, he only spent six months in Oakland while he was attending Saint Mary's College High School in Berkeley. I would drop him at the Bay Area Rapid Transit (BART) station on my way to work and pick him up there after school. Most of his classmates lived in Berkeley, and he had little opportunity to have a social life or participate in afterschool activities, since he was too young to apply for a driver's license.

He was feeling lonely and unhappy. I could see it was hard for him, but I thought that, with some effort on both of our parts, he would readjust in time. It was a surprise when he talked to me about moving to Santa Monica to live with his dad. He gave me all his reasons, which I understood and accepted as being legitimate. And yet, my heart was heavy, and my mind couldn't quite wrap around the possibility that once he moved to his dad's home, my son and I would not again live under the same roof, except for brief vacations.

Since the day I had held him in my arms for the first time, I had lived up to my promise that I would prepare him and myself for that day when he had the presence of mind and heart to pursue his own destiny. As a child, every time I put him on a plane to Mexico, it was with the sure conviction that the whole experience was good for him, and it was. As for me, I would go about my life every summer without him with a hole in my heart, which was filled again the moment I stepped off the plane in Mexico and saw him again, then brought him back home with me.

The time for his leaving home had arrived three years earlier than I expected, with its bundle of contradictory emotions—much too soon, much too abruptly. Knowing that he needed to be closer to his dad at that time in his life, to get to know his brothers and to live the high school experience the way he wanted and was best for him, I helped him pack the things he would take with him. Perhaps because my son was heading to Los Angeles in the morning, I thought of "I, Sarah Berhane" and her son. And I hoped and prayed her cousin in Los Angeles had really been able to keep him and had given him a home. I would never know.

The next morning Arturo left for Los Angeles. I drove him to the airport and stayed there watching the jet taxi out and take off. I stared into the open sky for a long time after it had disappeared in the misty layers of an overcast winter day in Oakland. All the way home I pushed back the tears, telling myself that tears were a luxury I couldn't afford, as I had told myself so many times in my life when faced with precarious emotional and financial situations. Arturo would be all right, and I would cope in time. By the time I arrived home, I had a sore throat. Sure that I had caught a cold, I made some chicken soup while I waited for the phone call from Arturo to let me know he'd arrived safely at his dad's home in Santa Monica. I sat down in the dining room, spooning chicken broth in, but I couldn't stomach it. I relaxed a bit when he finally called. I went down the hall to the bathroom. I passed the open door to his room. I pulled it shut.

Two hours later, my body was seized by chills and my temperature rose to a low fever. I'd had the good sense to prepare substitute lessons for that Thursday Arturo left and for the next day. I spent Friday and Saturday wrapped in a blanket, sleeping on the sofa in the living room. During moments of brief awareness, I was conscious that it was my spirit which ailed. My body was reacting to the grief in the only way it could, by forcing me to fight for its survival. Sunday afternoon, my body temperature was normal and my stomach tolerated some of the chicken soup. I took a very warm, invigorating shower and felt better.

Toward the evening, I walked into Arturo's room and sat at his desk, knowing that I would draw from a poem the strength I needed to transcend my crisis. But I didn't write a poem. Instead, I began with "Dear Luz." Hours later I finished the letter that brought great comfort and peace to my ailing spirit. I signed it, "Lucha." I smiled at the irony, amid the tears rolling down my face, dripping onto and wetting the back of my hand still holding the pen. I knew then which name I had chosen to be mine for the rest of my life.

Once and for all times, mispronounced or said as it was intended, the name I would take when I finally became a citizen was and would remain Lucha Corpi.

CONFESSIONS OF A BOOK BURNER

AFTER WE MOVED TO SAN LUIS POTOSÍ, every December, like the swallows, we returned to our town in Veracruz. With two exceptions, every year we spent our winter break with my grandmother and my aunt Pancha's family, and many other relatives and friends in Jáltipan. We also visited the Constantinos in Acayucan, my mother's relatives.

Jáltipan was a colonial town, with a history pre-dating the conquest of Mexico by the Spaniards. Long *corredores*— arcades—stood about a half-meter above street level and ran the length of each block in the center of town. They provided shelter from the sun for pedestrians and kept houses cool during the day. They also provided families or friends with a place to gather in the evenings to enjoy the breeze, tell stories, play and sing, and catch up on the latest news. Many streets were covered with pressed coarse sand, which allowed the water on stormy days to filter down and the excess to run off without creating much of a muddy mess on the main thoroughfares.

Welcomed by all in town were the cooler breezes of late fall, before the winter storms emptied a few more buckets of rain on the town again, and the northern winds blew the metal sheets off the roof at the market place, already loosened up by the mighty gales of summer. The event had become a yearly ritual—a challenge issued by the god of wind and tempests, and accepted by the townsmen in charge of rebuilding the roof.

"Why don't they just build a stronger roof?" I asked my dad when we saw the men working.

"Hmm. It isn't that easy."

"Why is it so hard?"

"We know nature may do the same thing year after year. Nature is cyclical, do you understand?"

I replied with a nod.

"So that means that we might know what's going to happen next year. But the tools we have to defend or protect ourselves aren't good enough yet."

"Abuelita Nico says that there are signs that tell when bad things are going to happen. She says we have to learn to read the signs. Like, when there's going to be an earthquake, all the animals hide. The birds are very quiet. And the sky is full of funny looking clouds. Is that true?"

"That's true. My mom is right."

"So why can't we also hide?"

"We can't hide from an earthquake. No one can. Not even the birds. The earthquake might happen any time, but we still have to be prepared for it all the time."

"Why can't we do something about the roof, then?"

"We don't have the materials to make the roof stronger. One day we will. In the meantime, we have to be ready to repair it when the tiles get blown away."

Despite the marketplace roof business, for most people in town, December was the best time in Jáltipan because it was almost a full month devoted to both, reverence and revelry, religious fervor and pagan festivity. Every year, we looked forward to seeing our friends and relatives and joining in the children's fiestas. In addition to posadas, Christmas and New Year's celebrations, we also celebrated my mom's, my dad's and my brother Miguel Ángel's birthdays.

My mother, who was an excellent baker and confectioner, insisted on making the birthday cakes, which was fine with us, knowing they'd be scrumptious. After Epiphany on the sixth of January, we always started back to San Luis to get ready for the beginning of a new school year. As we left, I was certain that our lives, like events in nature, were cyclical, too. We would all make it back in December to this town that had survived for a thousand years and would endure another millennium.

Even before we moved to San Luis, the topic of conversation had to do mostly with the large sulfur deposits in Jáltipan, which were estimated at about twenty million tons. When we arrived in town in December 1955, the Pan American Sulfur Company from Texas and Mexico's Gulf Sulfur Company had been formally contracted to install a sulfur extraction plant. National recruitment of skilled laborers and chemical and structural engineers had begun.

Many people in town favored the project and argued that Jáltipan would finally stop being a farming and cattle-raising community and join the twentieth century as an industrialized town. It was the way of progress, and the people in our town deserved it. Others argued that progress always came with a tag attached to it, and in this case no one had bothered to find out what people in town would have to pay for the privilege of joining the industrial age. But the plant had opened, and it seemed useless for anyone to oppose what was pretty much a fait accompli.

In December 1956, as soon as we rode into Jáltipan, our nostrils were assaulted by a penetrating, stifling smell. Next we noticed that some streets were covered by a carpet of green leaves. From time to time, we saw birds lying dead on the ground. The sight of fallen birds in itself wasn't strange. During the dog days of summer, when heat and humidity were extreme and almost unbearable, we had seen small birds faint and fall to the ground. Some of them would recover and fly to the nearest tree; others would never fly again. But this phenomenon could not be caused by the extreme heat, still seven months away. Closer to the street where Abuelita Nico and Aunt Pancha and her family lived, we also noticed many people who didn't look like they belonged in Jáltipan. "*Forasteros*—Newcomers," my dad said.

Later that day, sitting in the breezeway, the family talked about the new plant, which everyone called La Azufrera. The town had tripled its population in just a few years, and new workers kept coming from towns as far north and south as the northern and southern borders. The housing situation was precarious, even though the Azufrera management had a housing development close to the plant, but it only provided accommodations to the families of management officials and other professional staff, most of them North Americans. In town, it presented a money-making opportunity for restaurant owners and other people who could turn their homes into hostels or boarding houses, and for skilled laborers and domestic workers, but utility agencies were unable to provide services to everyone.

For two hours, between seven and nine every evening, the old alternator and generator at the electricity plant had to rest. The whole town was in darkness and people had to use candles and oil lamps. We children and young people loved this time of darkness. We got together to sing sometimes, and at others to play hide-and-seek and scare each other out of our wits at an abandoned haunted house. When I was twelve, one of those dark nights, I was on my way to my friend Marta's home. I felt the thrill of fingers gently brushing my hair, then lips brushing softly against mine. My hair stood on end, literally! I had just been kissed, but by whom? I was out of breath thinking that perhaps it was *el diablo* who had finally come to whisper sweet-nothings in my ear. I turned around and began to run home. I heard someone whistling a tune softly behind me, and I ran faster.

I was glad to see my grandmother, sitting in the breezeway, next to the front door and humming her favorite songs to herself. The oil lamp in the living room shed light on half her face. I sat on the floor next to her. A short time later, I heard someone whistling the same tune the kissing spirit had, then I saw the silhouette of a man coming toward us. As he stepped in the light, I realized that the kissing spirit was one of my cousin's friends. I was relieved it hadn't been *el diablo*, who'd given me my first kiss and stirred in me sensations and feelings difficult not to think about from that moment on. He stopped to talk with my grandmother, briefly sneaking a look at me. He smiled and I, automatically, smiled back. I liked his smile and his sense of humor, whenever I overheard his and my cousin's stories or their recounting of their day's events.

When we heard the voices of women coming down the breezeway and already greeting my grandmother, he bid everyone goodnight. My mother came out of the house. The kissing spirit went down the steps to the sidewalk, and then crossed the street. I saw him disappear in the semidarkness on the other side. Even if he and I were never again alone, I would always remember that first kiss.

After a while my attention finally shifted back to the women's conversation. Two of the women were complaining about the nightly power outages in town. The state and local officials weren't doing enough to remedy the situation. Surely, someone had to do something about them. My grandmother didn't complain. There were things happening in town that were worse than a couple of hours in the dark. When the electricity was back on, everyone went back to their respective homes.

My grandmother was right. There were worse things than the daily blackouts. The worst were the mineral waste fires. Apparently, to reach the underground deposits, extremely hot water had to be pumped in, then extracted and poured into large ponds where the sulfur would float to the surface and be collected. Since the water came out with dirt and other impurities in it, the solid waste was dumped on a special site, where it awaited to be disposed of by removal equipment and dump trucks. Because it still contained enough sulfur and other minerals in it, a waste pile would catch on fire every so often. Nothing could be done to contain the toxic pyre, so it burned until exhaustion. The breeze blew the toxic smoke all over town and the surrounding area, making the trees to shed their leaves and the birds to drop to the ground dead. It caused vehicles and metal equipment to rust faster. And it sent older parishioners in town to take refuge in the church, running from the "Smell of Hell" as noted in The Scriptures. They prayed to God that the town would be delivered from this evil.

When we children were already in bed, I heard my parents talking. "Imagine, Toya, there must be large empty holes, like caverns, underground," my father told my mom. I could hear the consternation in his voice but I didn't grasp the significance of his concern. Three years later, sadly I would.

An average of 1,800 to 2,000 tons a day, totaling up to 12 million tons had been extracted since the opening of La Azufrera. Soon, the Mexican government nationalized the industry and La Azufrera became a Mexican enterprise in its entirety. But the damage to the environment was already visible in agricultural fields that would not yield crops for a very long time. The large creeks, with crystalline ponds where we used to swim, were contaminated, and fish and other wildlife were dying in droves. All that polluted water poured into the Coatzacoalcos River and eventually joined the already oil-contaminated waters of the Gulf of Mexico. Under the town, there were now immense man-made caverns.

Sometime in the pre-dawn hours of August 26, 1959, our hometown Jáltipan de Morelos, Veracruz, suffered a 7.0 earthquake; the epicenter was located between our hometown and the neighboring town of Acayucan. Twenty people lost their lives or were injured. The temblor had damaged some structures in Acayucan, where my mom's relatives lived. There were a few injured and two dead in Jáltipan, but the town had been flattened by the furious seismic activity. Most of the homes were uninhabitable, and only a few structures had apparently been left undamaged.

That morning, one of my dad's friends at the telegraph office in Jáltipan managed to send a message to him in San Luis, informing him that my grandmother and the rest of the family were homeless for the time being, but no one was physically injured. If it was any consolation to him, our former home was one of the few still standing. My parents had built it with great care, making sure that it had deep foundations and strong walls to withstand the brute force of a killer quake. And it had. But the town was in ruins.

Gone was the whitewashed, colonial architecture of front porches, arcades with red tile roofs along the street. My grandmother's house and the Aguirre's home, where my brother Víctor, my sister Conchita and I had been born, were piles of rubble.

The church bell tower had collapsed. It had withstood the repeated furious assault of lightning bolts and torrential rains during countless hurricane seasons. Now it was broken in half, as if an angry King Kong had snapped its head off, chewed it and spat it out.

Silent were the *jaranas*, the guitars, the harps, the sound of the clay flutes and the drums that used to announce the coming of holidays. Somewhere under piles of bricks were the *güiros* and maracas. The rhythms of the marimbas everyone had danced to and my dad loved would no longer be heard. Hushed, too, were the voices of the singers, the poets and the storytellers. Strewn around the shoes of the fandango dancers, who for generations had danced on portable wooden platforms in the town's main square, from dusk to dawn every Friday.

The townspeople's shattered dreams for a brighter future were buried underneath layers of debris and damaged personal belongings. In fact, physically, this town my father loved so dearly had ceased to exist. I, too, mourned for this magical community where I was formed and given the tools I would need to survive throughout my life, and where I had learned to thread verses and tell stories.

The spirit of the people, the native Jaltipanecos, remained intact, however. It grew even stronger as the painful labor of clearing up the debris and rebuilding the town began. The new Jáltipan went up anew very fast, in part because of the quick intervention of the governor of Veracruz, who was one of Jáltipan's "native sons." His staff and other state officials made it possible for people to get low-interest loans to rebuild their homes. The Eminent Domain act went into effect and the government bought at minimum cost the land where the porches and arcades had been so streets could be widened and paved. Square-shaped houses made of brick and cement went up everywhere; they no longer had high ceilings to keep them cool. Those who could afford it had small porches built with wrought ironwork to allow ventilation and block access to intruders. But the level of noise had gone up a few decibels everywhere.

Being in poor health and needing surgery for an abdominal hernia, my grandmother came to live with us in San Luis. She survived the operation, and I slept in her room for months so I could assist her during the night. I was in dentistry school and taking a course on anatomy as part of the curriculum. I had the bones of a full skeleton in a burlap sack in the closet. I had to study the bones and know the names of each of them, as well as every muscle and ligament that would attach to them to make motion possible. I had to keep the sack in my room upstairs because my grandmother, understandably, couldn't bear having them in the room we shared. Sometimes I fell asleep, lulled by the sound of the old tunes she hummed, and in the early morning I would wake up to her whispering voice. Her presence in my life was of great comfort to me.

I went back to Jáltipan after the earthquake, when I was sixteen, three years before I got married and moved to Berkeley. My brother Víctor and Cuca Berrones, a good friend and classmate from San Luis, had made the trip with me. We were staying at the home of the Ortiz-Guerrero family, who had been my parents' best friends. We and the Ortiz children had grown up together, and Marta was one of my best friends. The next morning, before everyone else arose I got up, dressed and went out. I walked around, trying to figure out where everything I'd known before had been. Memories flooded as I saw our childhood home still standing as a monument to my parents' boundless spirit and love for us. I didn't want to disturb the occupants; instead I walked on, curious to find out if the grocery where we had bought chewing gum, candy and firecrackers every December still existed. It didn't. I walked past the main square and looked at the new church for awhile, then ended up on a wide sandy path that seemed unfamiliar to me. It led to El Cerro de la Malinche, a mound named after Malintziín Tenepal, the native Mexican woman who aided Hernán Cortés in his conquest of Mexico in the sixteenth century. She was also known as La Malinche and as Marina, her baptismal name when she converted to Catholicism.

For having helped the conqueror, she had been reviled as a traitor to her race through the ages. Any Mexican who in some way or another was believed to be a traitor to the homeland was called a "Malinchista," including those who left Mexico to live abroad. She had also become a symbolic Madre de la Raza—Mother of the Mestizo Race. Octavio Paz called her *la gran chingada*, the most maligned and infamous of the Mexican women, who had been raped by Cortés, used and abused by his captains and their conquering army. Although Malinche was at times praised for her astuteness and her facility with languages, she was pejoratively referred to as La Gran Puta—the great whore—or Cortés' whore.

Before the conquest, together with other neighboring towns, Jáltipan had been part of the large Coatzacoalcos region. The old folks in town swore that Malinche was buried in that mound, that her body had been brought back to her birthplace for her eternal rest. As children, we had also heard the story of Malinche and the claim that she had actually been born close by. I had also watched the elders in town perform the "Baile de la Malinche—Dance of La Malinche," which was a reenactment of the first meeting between Aztec Emperor Moctezuma Xocoyotzin and Hernán Cortés. Malintzín Tenepal stood a few steps back, but between the two men, as the link between the old and the new worlds, translating Nahuatl and Spanish. Men dressed as Spanish soldiers or Aztec warriors also reenacted the siege of Tenochtitlan.

I walked around the mound a few times, despite the polite but curious looks of passersby for whom I was just another tourist. I was in awe, for, in the midst of destruction and strife, El Cerro de la Malinche stood as a monument to the enduring spirit of the people in my hometown. Learning more about this woman, who had defied the sociopolitical and cultural canons of both the new and the old world, became one of my goals from that moment on.

I would remember that episode of my youth again after I became a student at U.C. Berkeley. Like every Chicano and Chicana in the early seventies, I had read Octavio Paz's *Laberinto de la soledad*—*The Labyrinth of Solitude*. But as much as I could understand the author's take on the story of La Malinche, I didn't quite agree with his views. Later, I enrolled in an independent study course, supervised by Chicano Studies Professor Velia García-Hancock, who was gathering background materials to teach the first course on La Chicana. My project involved writing a term paper contrasting the lives of Mesoamerican women and Spanish women during and after the conquest, with a bibliography of publications that would help Professor García-Hancock prepare for the course. I spent countless hours in the U.C. libraries. Not surprisingly, I found very few books and publications on this particular subject. At the end of the quarter, I turned my paper and the bibliography in and passed the course.

My fascination with Malinche and her life, however, was renewed. My friend Roberta Orona had also developed an interest in her, and we had both begun a search for books and materials that would give us clues as to who this enigmatic but very maligned woman had really been. On my next trip to Mexico, I went into many bookstores in Mexico City, looking for books on the legendary Malinche. I walked into a bookstore at the Mexico City Zócalo, approached the counter, where two men asked how they could help me.

"Do you have any books about La Malinche?" I asked.

The younger of the two gave me a confused look, then asked the older man, "*¿Quién es La Malinche?*—Who's La Malinche?"

The older man looked at me, arched a brow and then replied, "La Malinche was the wh . . . the girlfriend of Hernán Cortés, conqueror of Mexico."

¡Por favor! I couldn't help chuckle. He and I knew exactly what he had meant to say—the *puta, the whore*—not the girlfriend. He blushed and rushed to the back of the store to help the young man find something, anything, so I could get out of there. They returned with a worn-out, browning, used book on the conquest of Mexico. By the looks of it, the tome could well have been published back in the sixteenth century. I knew there would be little on La Malinche in that text, as was the case in most Mexican history books. It was so inexpensive that I bought it anyway. Before I returned to Berkeley, I did manage to find two slim volumes with some interesting facts but also full of speculation about the person and life of "the mother of the race."

Upon my return to Berkeley, I shared my experience at the bookstore with Roberta. That night, as I did every night about ten o'clock, I sat at my table and began my nightly ritual of writing my innermost thoughts to make sense of my life. At the end of every session, I would crumple the sheets of paper, throw them in the fireplace, light them and watch them burn.

That night something different was happening. As soon as I held the pencil in my hand, words started trickling out but finally grew to a cascade on the paper. Past midnight, I held in my hand a long poem in four sections I had titled "Los poemas de Marina—The Marina Poems." It spoke about Malintzín Tenepal, La Malinche. As I read the whole poem aloud, I realized that, for the first time, I had transcended my immediate reality and stepped into a different space, a territory unknown and yet familiar, where everything was possible. I felt exhilarated and elated at once.

I reached for the phone to share my poems with my Panamanian friend Berta Ramona Thayer. Like me, she was a night owl and was probably getting ready for bed about then. When she answered, I immediately said that I wanted to read something to her and without delay I read the poems to her. I waited for her to say something, but there was only silence at the other end. Assuming that I had wakened her up and that my reading had lulled her back to sleep, I began to apologize. I would call her the next day.

"No, no, don't hang up. Read them again," she said.

After I finished the second reading, she didn't comment on the poems, telling me instead that she wanted me to meet a friend and she would be calling me the next day with a day and time for the appointment.

"Bring your poem," she said and hung up.

That night, past midnight, match in hand, I contemplated burning one of the drafts of the poems, but I could not do it. A couple of days later, Berta picked the poems up and took them to her friend Catherine Rodríguez-Nieto. A meeting was scheduled and Berta took my son Arturo and me to Catherine's home in Oakland. When we walked in, Arturo went to Catherine immediately and said hello. Catherine turned to me and said, "You're the 'magic boy's mother!" I was confused. She explained that she and Arturo had met before and had had a very nice chat at a lecture given by a Mexican shaman on campus all of us had attended. She wasn't interested in the shaman's talk and saw Arturo in a corner of the room, drawing, and went to talk with him. There was I, the magic boy's mother and the poet she had looked forward to meeting. I nodded at a vague recollection of a tall woman, talking with Arturo that night.

Catherine explained to us that she was working with three other women at Berkeley on translations of poems written by women poets who worked in languages other than English but who lived in the United States. Norton was going to publish the anthology. And she hoped I would give her permission to translate the poems and perhaps go over her translations with her. She later confessed that all the while she kept mentally begging God that I would choose her as my translator. I agreed. How could I not, I also told her later. There was something magical about our first meeting, something that felt right from the moment I walked in, as if it had been meant to happen all along. Destiny at work, I thought.

Cathy asked to see my other poems. From then on, once a week, over a glass of wine, while we reviewed the translations and talked, Cathy and I became the best of friends, as did our families as well. Although I never asked for her husband Alcides' help or hers, they had the uncanny ability to know when I needed it and did for Arturo and me without my having to ask. I learned from them and my friend Berta what true friendship was meant to be.

"The Marina Poems" were published in the Norton anthology. For the next ten years after their publication, I wrote nothing but poetry, every night, from ten to midnight, when everything was ready for the next day, my son asleep and concentration was possible. Sometimes, the poems wouldn't come together, and I burned the drafts. One night I decided not to do it. I threw them instead in the garbage can on the side of house. Unable to fall asleep that night, I got up two hours later. At the risk of being mugged or worse, I went downstairs, retrieved the papers and burned them in the fireplace. As I was finally falling asleep, I wondered about this idiosyncrasy, this compelling need to watch the poems go up in flames, but the reasons for this unusual, perhaps morbid, behavior escaped me.

Unexpectedly, I experienced a two-year long poetic pause. Every night I sat at my table and every night I ended up with balls of crumpled paper all around my chair. My heart felt heavy as I gathered the paper balls and burned them. But burning them wasn't enough to make me sleep well. I had no idea that poetic silences happen naturally to all poets. It's simply the time when we need to find a new spring to renew and replenish the well of creativity. Perhaps it wasn't writing poetry but simply writing that was important, I thought. So just to keep myself from going mad and to heal a stomach ulcer I'd developed during that period, I began to write stories. One of those stories developed into a much longer work, and I wrote *Delia's Song*, my first novel and my first work in English. In time, my poetry creative well was replenished. Every so often I would reach for "The Poems of Marina," to revisit the moment I discovered I was and had been meant to be a poet in this world.

Just like all my lifelong good friends, La Malinche, ever present in my spirit, has been with me through the lean years and times of plenty in my life, through poetic silences and the emergence of new voices in me. Most of all, she has been my companion down the unfamiliar paths and trails I have sometimes willfully chosen to walk in search of my destiny: the roads taken.

One of those roads led me to the fulfillment of a childhood dream, to write a mystery novel. In 1989, during a sojourn in California's Sierra Nevada, I first briefly saw and heard Chicana P.I. Gloria Damasco, the lead detective in a series of novels I was to write, and the woman who would eventually tell La Malinche's story in *Black Widow's Wardrobe*, the third in the series of four Gloria Damasco detective novels.

I had gone to the Sierra Nevada specifically to revise and organize my second poetry manuscript, *Variaciones sobre una tempestad / Variations on a Storm*, which was already due at the press. The late Ted and Pee Wee Kalman, whom I had met through Cathy and Alcides, offered me their condo for a week in the town of Donner Lake, a short drive from Lake Tahoe. I accepted. A good thing was that my good friend and publisher at Third Woman Press, Norma Alarcón, and her husband, visited me there for a couple of days, and we had a chance to talk about the project. Then they went on to explore the Lake Tahoe area on their way back to Oakland.

At the end of three days of intense work, my manuscript was ready. I put back in a folder the photocopies of loose poems that I had decided not to include in the collection. One by one, I burned the extra Xerox copies of all the poems, but not of Cathy's translations. I also threw in the pyre all those poems that I didn't consider to be good enough for inclusion in the collection, or to keep in the unpublished work folder. I was done, but since I had the condo for two more days, I decided to stay and get some rest.

I had taken with me some CDs, among them a recording of the Puccini opera *Madame Butterfly*. I am not an opera buff, but for some unknown reason, I was obsessed with that opera, especially the aria "Un Bel Di." I had also started a list of books I wanted to read about the architecture, viticulture and the wine industry in the Napa and Sonoma Valleys, also known as the California Wine Country. Before my stay in Donner Lake, I had made repeated trips to both valleys, looking into the history of the Vallejo family in Sonoma and the Peralta family in Oakland. Following my obsessions at the time, I had frequently driven to Los Angeles to study gangs and the events that led to a riot during the 1970 National Chicano Moratorium. I was also researching an elixir I had come across during a visit with my son, when he spent his junior year abroad in Brazil. I had already decided to write my first mystery novel, *Eulogy for a Brown Angel*, and sensed, more than knew, that all of my obsessions and interests had to do with the plotting of the novel. Yet, I had no idea how they would eventually fit together, nor had I conceived my main character, the detective that would need access to all that knowledge and experience.

Looking to research some of these topics during my sojourn in the mountains, I paid a fruitless visit to a local bookstore in Lake Tahoe. I bought instead a P.D. James mystery novel and drove back to Donner Lake. After a walk along the lake shore, I went back to the condo when dark heavy clouds began to gather above the mountains. Sunset was still two hours away. I locked the sliding doors to the lake before I went up the spiral staircase to the living area.

I turned on my CD player and listened to Puccini's opera, then lay down on the sofa to read P.D. James' mystery yarn. About an hour later, I slipped into a deep sleep, only to be awakened later by a loud noise. I opened my eyes to total darkness. I was sure someone was in the sleeping area downstairs. My fears immediately raced down the spiral staircase to the sliding doors. Had I locked them, after all? Was someone down there, lurking, waiting? How long before the intruder made his way up the spiral staircase?

I listened intently, but all I could hear and feel were my intermittent breaths and the rapid beating of my heart. I was trembling from head to toe, but I forced myself to sit up while I weighed the risks of going downstairs and confronting the intruder. My eyes adjusted to the darkness and, as quietly as possible, I walked to the fireplace and got hold of the poker. I began my descent, barefoot, taking one step and deep breath at a time. I stood at the foot of the stairs and surveyed the area, then walked to the sliding doors and checked them. They were locked. I looked behind each closet and room door and under each bed until I was satisfied no one was there.

As I got to the top of the stairs, my heart did a Mexican hat dance in my chest. Something or someone, a white raggedy gown on, its arms flailing wildly, swayed and gestured just outside the sliding doors to the dark balcony.

"It's not of this world," I thought. My heart picked up its pace. The phantasm went on with its macabre dancing. I put down the poker and looked around for a cross or a crucifix. I sucked in a nervous chuckle as I realized that I would not find such an object there. My friends, the Kalmans, were Jewish. In the absence of a ghost-busting instrument, I crossed one index finger over the other to make a cross and walked closer to the sliding doors. The specter turned out to be a large white windsock, dancing in the night air. I had no idea who had hung it from a branch of the pine next to the balcony during my long nap. I dropped to the floor, scared out of my wits. Still shaking and breathing hard, I made myself a cup of coffee and sat in an easy chair, cloaked in a cotton blanket and darkness, unable to close my eyes and get some sleep.

Closer to dawn, I turned on the CD player, low, hoping that *Madame Butterfly* would lull me to sleep. It took a long while for the soprano to reach the first heart-wrenching phrases of the aria "Un Bel Di," and for my eyes to finally close for what seemed only seconds. As if on a light red screen inside my lids, I saw a pair of dark hands and arms and, nestled between them, a little boy, a toddler, who appeared to be asleep.

"I am Gloria. And this child is for you," a woman's voice said as she handed me the little boy. I extended my arms to receive her gift. They were still outstretched when I opened my eyes. I heard the crack of thunder in the distance, the same noise that had awakened me the previous night. It was noon and the thunderstorm was moving in. It would soon be raging right above Donner Lake. Driving down the mountain in such unsettled weather made no sense. I made lunch and ate. Then I picked up my notebook and wrote: "Luisa and I found the child lying on his side in a fetal position." This is the opening line of *Eulogy for a Brown Angel*, my first Gloria Damasco mystery novel.

In time, I learned that Gloria possessed some sort of psychic power. Was she a kind of fortune teller? Palm reader, perhaps? Did she delve in Black or White Magic? Maybe she was a healer, then again maybe a sorceress. Was she a New Age or Old Age psychic? There was so much to research. I dove into the psychic pool without hesitation.

Norma Alarcón, my very willing partner in psychic and other crime research, and I attended countless psychic fairs and séances, and had private consultations with psychics specializing in regression to past lives. We quickly learned to tell whether the spirits at a séance or spiritualist session would appear in full view or be a no-show and simply disappear with our money. We compared notes and laughed at the goings-on during the sessions on our way back home.

Sometimes on my own, I attended mid-summer and mid-winter solstice celebrations. There were always bonfires out in the open or fires burning in safe containers. Fascinated, I sat and watch the pyres burn. I had my fortune read many times, my aura cleansed at least twice. I attempted astral projection, but my reptilian brain refused to let my spirit soar freely. I learned the techniques for channeling and regression to past lives and used them on Norma, then on my friend Carlos Gonzales, whom I would marry in 1994. Later, with some intriguing results, I also tried the techniques on my most trusted writer friends, always in the presence of their witnesses, who would record everything said and done during the sessions.

Although I believed that most people were sincere in their beliefs that they possessed an extrasensory gift, all in all, I only came across two and perhaps three psychics that impressed me as truly having a "dark gift," an extrasensory perception. A man who read the cards for me at a psychic fair in Berkeley never asked a question, which many of the other readers did to extract information from the clients, use it to impress them and justify the cost of the session. He told me I was very far from home and had no family in Berkeley. He described my problematic relationship with my mother until my father's death. I had a highly developed intuition, but I did not trust my hunches enough. My relationship with my friend (Carlos) was not going anywhere until I examined my doubts and expectations about marriage. He advised me to take my time before I made a decision to buy a house. As with most predictions, one can only confirm their veracity once they happen, so the whole business of buying a home, which as a woman with a single salary I could not easily do, seemed irrelevant. But later, when circumstances changed and I looked into buying a house, his advice made sense. I sensed that he was a psychic reader, who used the cards as tools.

The second was a woman, who specialized in readings of the aura and cleansing of chakras, by sensing the heat emitted from the body and reworking the body's energy with her hands. Her technique reminded me of the one used by practitioners of the Japanese healing art of Reiki, although she did my body reading while I was standing up. She never touched me, never tried to gather information about past or present ailments, either emotional or physical. As she worked and reworked my energy to realign my chakras, every so often I would hear a creaking of a bone in my skull, my sternum, my spine and my left hip joint. She concentrated her energy again around my head and talked about my abundant mental energy (red in my aura), which at times seemed to drown my emotions (green in my aura) and how difficult it had been for me to finally strike a balance between them. She said that my stomach was the organ that recorded my emotions and reacted to them. As a poet, I found her comments prosaic and doubtful. Then again, I'd had an ulcer, which although healed, had left me with a very sensitive stomach. I finally had to admit she was right when she told me it was the most vulnerable organ in my body. I walked out believing that she had a special gift.

The psychic that most impressed me, however, was a man at a mantic arts fair in San Francisco. My niece Frieda Molina and I had gone to see the first Tut exhibit at the old De Young Museum in Golden Gate Park. We had parked on a street behind the Academy of Sciences building and the large esplanade between the museum and the academy. On summer Sundays, people picnicked there while they listened to free symphony and opera concerts. Being late spring, the esplanade was usually empty, but not this time, as a mantic-arts fair had set up shop there. And I thought, "Hmm. Research time!"

I asked Frieda if she would be willing to explore "the occult" with me after seeing the exhibit at the museum, and she agreed. So, two hours later we each got tickets for our individual psychic fair selections and agreed to a meeting time and place.

My first ticket went to a man who specialized in astral projection and talked about Shirley MacLaine's book on that particular subject. I couldn't fly on my own even in my dreams, let alone while awake. After unsuccessfully trying a few times, I thanked him and left. I went into another tent where a man did psychic readings of past lives. But when he began to talk about a mischievous spirit that had decided to hang from my left ear, my incredulity antenna went up. He closed his eyes and gestured in the air around my ear, then said: "Done. He's gone." I thanked him and left. I slid my fingers down the edge of my earlobe to get rid of any filament remaining, not from the spirit, but from the spurious ghost-busting psychic.

I walked to a tent at the very end of the row. A sign said, "Do not enter until called." A couple of minutes later, a woman came out. She seemed distracted and brushed against my arm as she went past me, without an apology or a look in my direction. Oh-uh, that bad, I thought. I heard the voice of a man calling me in, and my heart began to beat a bit harder. I took a deep breath, let it out slowly and walked in.

The man had his eyes closed and pointed to the chair across the table from him. Without uttering a word, I sat down and put my slip in the ticket basket. With his eyes still closed, he leaned forward, dropped his head and rested his lower right arm on the table, with the palm of his hand open to me. He described a space in my house where there were lots of books, then another place in front of a large window where I sat at a table, writing something. The scene shifted and he saw me throwing loose pages of books, perhaps, or maybe sheets of paper with something written on them onto a smoking pyre. I had once been a man who had written on those papers, but he couldn't explain why exactly I was burning them—perhaps disappointment, perhaps trying to keep them from an enemy who would use what I wrote against me. So I was a man then, not a woman, who had traveled to that place from afar. As that man, I spoke with an accent but the psychic didn't know where I came from or where that pyre was. Then, he was silent for a few seconds. "Beware," he said, and lowered his hand, letting it rest palm down on the table. I knew the session was over. I left, not having exchanged one word with him.

I met my niece Frieda and we walked to the car. She told me about her session, and I talked about mine with the ghost-busting psychic and the astral traveling guy, and we laughed. It was almost dark when I got home. The first thing I saw was the basket next to the fireplace, where I had balls of crumpled paper with fragments of poems started but not finished. I piled the paper balls onto the fireplace grate, set them on fire and watched them burn as I thought about the psychic's vision. I had probably been a book burner, although I had burned my own as well as other people's writings. This certainly explained my obsessive habit of burning my poems. The "beware" part confounded me. I had once burned my hand when I picked up a ball of burning paper that rolled off the pile on the grate. But that was neither here nor there when it came to a warning in my present life. Fire fascinated me, but I was always careful around it.

As I started to write *Eulogy for a Brown Angel,* I realized that Gloria Damasco was a clairvoyant, someone who had visions about the future. I had heard people talk about poets as visionaries, and I agreed with the description. Although I was sure my sister Conchita had the gift of clairvoyance, to make sure I was on the right track, I decided to research the subject of extrasensory perceptions and read about well-known psychics. I asked all my friends if anyone knew a clairvoyant in the Bay Area. No one did. One night, as I closed my eyes, I heard Gloria's voice say something in Spanish, followed by her laughter. There was something familiar about her voice in Spanish and the way she laughed. It should have been obvious to me who Gloria was in my real life, but at the moment I was still sure that she was a product of my imagination. The next morning, the first person I immediately thought about was my biological sister, Conchita, who had always amazed me with her predictions and visions. In many ways both of them were different, but they both shared a dark gift, a way of seeing that most people, and certainly I, did not have.

Eventually, through my friend, the novelist María Espinosa, I was able to contact a clairvoyant and I went to see her. Sally didn't trust writers, but because María had recommended me, she agreed to meet with me. Although at first she was quite reluctant to talk about her gift, she soon opened up, and we had a wonderful talk. She confirmed what I knew about clairvoyance and the way visions came to her and how she interpreted them. She had worked with the police many times to locate missing persons, dead or alive. By then, *Eulogy* had been published and I left a copy with her. She called me a week later to tell me I had been very successful in describing Gloria's vision.

Although I still read books about reincarnation, other mantic arts and clairvoyance, that session marked the end of my delving into the mantic arts. In each of the novels, Gloria tries to explain for herself and to the rest of us what her dark gift is all about. About it, she says:

" . . . I had never been able to save anyone whose life, in my visions, was fated to end. It bothered me no end to see what fatal blow destiny had in store for someone yet be unable to prevent it. But that was the nature of this dark gift, this extrasensory prescience in me—*la otra*.

"Most people did not understand what clairvoyance was. My visions weren't a tidied bunch of related scenes laid out, like a classic story, in a linear narrative. They varied from images to smells and sounds that bombarded my dreams. My subconscious somehow sorted them out and stored them until, if ever, I worked on a related case."

As a poet, I understood well the nature of her visions. Having a sister who had them helped. I still researched thoroughly every aspect of each novel, something my husband-to-be Carlos Medina Gonzales, my friends and relatives enjoyed to participate in from time to time. By the time Carlos and I got married, I was already doing research for *Black Widow's Wardrobe*, the third of the Gloria Damasco detective series. Carlos loved traveling with me to all the places where the action of the novels took place. I asked him to take photos of places and people engaged in certain activities that could become relevant later when I finally sat down to do the actual writing. He took photos of everything I pointed at, and then catalogued them for me for possible use as locales or important sites in the novels. He enjoyed being "my official photographer and cataloguer," and I was happy he could share in the research process since it was not possible for him to be involved in the writing of the novel.

Sometimes, my friend Norma Alarcón went with us on research trips. We were all compatible travelers and had a great time later comparing notes. Following my other obsessions, and although Norma couldn't go with us, we were looking forward to traveling to Coyoacán in México City to visit La casa de La Malinche, the Plaza de la Conchita across from it, and the chapel where Malintzín Tenepal—Marina—had prayed after she converted to Catholicism. We had also made plans to go to Cuernavaca and Tepoztlán, a neighboring town. I already knew that these places would be important, but I had no idea how.

By coincidence, my publisher and editor Nicolás Kanellos was in Cuernavaca with his family. We talked on the phone and he suggested I pay a visit to a very interesting church in Tepoztlán, the church of the Holy Trinity. I did. As soon as Carlos and I entered the town, I knew this was the place I had been looking for and the church of the Holy Trinity was one of the many sites I would need to be acquainted with before I returned to the States. After each visit to these places, I grew more and more intrigued about the possible connection between Licia Lecuona, the black widow, and the legendary Malinche. And I was eager to return to Oakland to begin writing their stories and sate my curiosity.

As always, it was one of Gloria's visions that started the process of writing *Black widow's Wardrobe*. And in the case of Malinche's story, her vision was one of fire:

" . . . The fire flares up, and her hair catches on fire, then her clothes. The kitchen fills with the stink of searing flesh and hair. Terrified, I do nothing to help her. I watch her burn until there is nothing but a pile of smoking bones. I flee into the darkness, and run and run until I can go no more."

I immediately thought about the psychic who told me to be wary of fire. Perhaps this was what he was referring to, then again perhaps not. In this case, I guessed from the very first of her visions that Gloria was ready to tell the story of La Malinche, and I wrote it.

In some way, Gloria's visions form and inform the plot of every novel in the series. Her visions become my obsessions and concerns, and I follow them. But like Gloria, I also do my share of legwork, by doing my research thoroughly. I experience to the extent safely possible what I must write about, including the handling of firearms, so Gloria has everything she needs to solve the case at a moment's notice.

Seven years after *Black Widow's Wardrobe* was published, I would remember again the psychic's last word to me, "Beware." Our house in Oakland had caught on fire while we were in Stockton, attending the funeral and burial of Danny, Carlos' middle son. The fire was the culmination of six weeks in the summer of 2006, which had begun with the death of Guillermo Hernández, my first husband and my son Arturo's father, and two weeks later Danny's death. Carlos hadn't been feeling well. But the distress of seeing Danny dying and being the one who had authorized his doctor to disconnect his son's life support had aggravated his condition. His heart was beating so slow that he could die in his sleep. He had to be taken to the ER a second time in Stockton. Near midnight, we were at the hospital when Carla and Andy Arias, our next door neighbors and good friends, called to tell me that our house was on fire and the firefighters were there.

The electrical fire in our home had started in and consumed most of my library and spread fast through the wiring, requiring the destruction of walls and part of the ceiling to finally contain it. Almost everything in the house had been destroyed by the electrical fire, or damaged by its toxic smoke, or by the water. Craig Howard, my niece Frieda's husband, came to help and thanks to him every photo that he could find he collected and took home to clean and dry for us. I was very grateful for his gift to us.

Carlos needed a lot of rest, and finally a pacemaker had to be put in to regulate his heartbeat. I was left with the multitude of tasks involved in the reconstruction of our home. I also had to document every single loss for a very difficult insurance company, bent from the beginning on paying as little as possible for our losses. In order for them to pay for my signed first editions and other books in my collection, I had to make a list of everything contained in my library.

Three months after the fire, I stood on a pile of burned books and other materials and manuscripts that had been my library. My heart was beating fast and faster. It felt as if it would jump out of my mouth any second. I began to rake the mound of papers with my hand. I was looking for the first pages of all signed first editions that comprised one third of my literary collection. I was also digging in it for my personal papers, my poetry journals and some of my first poems. I was overwhelmed but I plowed through the remains.

As required by the insurance company, I began to list the signed first editions, including my own books, and looked through pages on the ground for the titles of other books in my library. As I searched through all the loose pages, some were half burned or so smoke-damaged that it was difficult to read them. But many were still legible.

I began to read and try to guess whose book it was the pages belonged to: Mark Greenside, Lorna Dee Cervantes, Francisco Alarcón, Ana Castillo, Alicia Gaspar de Alba, Sarah Cortez, Angela de Hoyos, Gloria Anzaldúa, Bárbara Brinson Pineda, J.P. Gutiérrez, Víctor Martínez, Rodrigo Reyes, Sandra Cisneros, Denise Chávez, Helena María Viramontes, María Herrera-Sobek, Michael Nava, Manuel Ramos, José Montoya, Norma E. Cantú, Claire Joysmith, Mary Helen Ponce, Norma Alarcón, Bernice Zamora, María Espinosa, Cherríe Moraga, Judith Ortiz Cofer, Margarita Cota Cárdenas, Inés Hernández, Pat Mora, Jesús S. Treviño, Ricardo Sánchez, Erlinda Gonzales-Berry, Abelardo Delgado, Montserrat Fontes, Tey Diana Rebolledo, Harriet Rohmer, Rudolfo Anaya, Arturo Islas, Rolando Hinojosa-Smith, Miguel Méndez, Victor Villaseñor, Jack and Adelle Foley, Rosemary Catácalos, Claire Ortalda, Floyd Salas, John Curl, Graciela Limón, Kim McMillon, Aurora Levins Morales, Margaret Shedd, Cecile Pineda, Estela Portillo-Trambley, Carmen Tafolla, Miriam Bornstein, Gary Soto, Daniel Chacón, Benjamín Alire Sáenz, Alfred Arteaga, Nina Serrano, Alejandro Murguía, Luis Valdez, Juvenal Acosta, Elsa Cross, Julia Vinograd and the Telegraph Avenue street poets, Neeli Cherkovski, Jack Hirshman and other North Beach poets, JoAnn Hernández, José Antonio Burciaga, Tino Villanueva, Juan Felipe Herrera, Alma Luz Villanueva, Roberta Fernández, Ishmael Reed and Tennessee Reed, Naomi Quiñónez, Sara Paretsky, Linda Grant, Janet Dawson, and many other Sisters-in-Crime.

Day after day, I sat there, among the smoked-stained pages from hundreds of books and anthologies by the many poets, writers, children's authors and crime writers I have been privileged to meet and have read through forty years as a poet and writer.

I wasn't alone any longer. Their words were my comfort, the quiet fire that kept my heart beating joyfully and my spirit soaring through endless days of grief postponed as I labored to put Carlos' and my life back together.

Tucked between two half-torn, smoky pages of the 1980-first edition of *Palabras de Mediodía / Noon Words*, my first poetry collection, I found a postcard of the elementary school I had attended in Jáltipan. My hometown had been devastated by an earthquake and now my home by fire. I looked at the postcard and remembered all the people now gone from the earth, who had had so much to do with who and what I am. I promised myself I would go back to Jáltipan one more time before I died and visit with my dear relatives and friends there, and especially with La Malinche in her mound grave. At that moment, I knew that, like the old book burner in the psychic's vision, I, too, would survive this disaster. And my poems and stories would once again rise from the ashes.

ACKNOWLEDGEMENTS

THROUGHOUT MY LIFE I have been the recipient of great love, encouragement and support from family and friends, students and teachers, storytellers and musicians, shamans and visionaries, editors and publishers, librarians and booksellers, and poets and writers—my boundless gratitude to each and all of them.

For their unwavering belief in and support of my work and my authorship and the gift of their friendship for over three decades at Arte Público Press, I especially acknowledge and thank Nicolás Kanellos, Founder and Director, and Gabriela Baeza Ventura, Executive Editor, also my editors for *Confessions*, as well as Marina Tristán, Assistant Director, and the loving and always helpful past and present staff at APP.

Mil gracias a María Herrera-Sobek, Mark Greenside, Carla Trujillo, Catherine Rodríguez-Nieto, Mimi Albert and María Espinosa, for their invaluable critique of earlier versions of some of these essays and their encouragement. Dulce María Franyutti Constantino for sharing with me a lifetime of family stories. René Renato Franyutti Constantino and Ricardo Perry for digital images of Jáltipan pre- and post-1959, archived at the Centro de Documentación del Son Jarocho. My heartfelt gratitude to Salvador Guereña and Callie Bowdish for patiently guiding me through the retrieval and downloading of family photos from the California Ethnic and Multicultural Archives collection at U.C. Santa Barbara. Special thanks to Oakland visual artist Patricia Rodríguez for "The Burning Heart" book cover art, and Norma Elia Cantú for allowing me to quote briefly from her snapshot, "The Stroller," in her book *Canícula: Snapshots of a Girlhood en la Frontera* (University of New Mexico Press, 1995).

~~~

Earlier versions of the following essays have appeared in various anthologies. I thank and credit the following publishers and editors herewith:

"Epiphany: The Third Gift," *Latina: Women's Voices from the Borderlands* (Simon & Schuster, 1995, Lillian Castillo-Speed, editor)

"Four, Free and Invisible," *Daughters of the Fifth Sun* (Riverhead Books, 1995, Bryce Milligan, Mary Guerrero-Milligan, and Angela de Hoyos, editors)

"La Página Roja," *The Other Latin@* (University of Arizona Press, 2011, Lorraine M. López and Blas Falconer, editors).